Also by Rick Johnson,
Invest Successfully and Protect Your Assets,
published by iUniverse 2004.

KEEP YOUR ASSETS
TAKE MY ADVICE

It is Easier to Climb Out of a Shallow Hole

RICK JOHNSON,
CASL™, CFP®, CMFC®, RFC®

iUniverse, Inc.
New York   Bloomington

Keep Your Assets. Take My Advice.
It is Easier to Climb Out of a Shallow Hole

Copyright © 2009 Rick Johnson

iUniverse books may be ordered through booksellers or by contacting:

iUniverse
1663 Liberty Drive
Bloomington, IN 47403
www.iuniverse.com
1-800-Authors (1-800-288-4677)

ISBN: 978-14401-2693-2 (pbk)
ISBN: 978-1-4401-2695-6 (cloth)
ISBN: 978-1-4401-2694-9 (ebk)

Printed in the United States of America

iUniverse rev. date: 3/12/2009

DEDICATION

This book is dedicated to my son Reese Cannon Johnson, my brother David Hillman Johnson, my best friend Michael Charles Rowland, and my dad Hillman Eugene Johnson. Their influence upon my life will last forever. They are forever in my heart.

I couldn't have written this book without the support of my very giving, thoughtful and beautiful wife Natalie, my highly intelligent and cool as all get out son Marshall and my sweet pumpkin love daughter Rudi.

CONTENTS

ACKNOWLEDGMENTS

I am not naïve enough to believe that I am in control of my life. Nor do I think for one moment that everything in this book came from my thoughts alone. It is an accumulation of what I have learned over the years.

These are the most important things in my life: Jesus Christ, my family, my friends, and those acquaintances that I can influence to lead a life based on conservative Christian values.

Many thanks go to Bruce Kelvington and Roger Shealy who gave me an opportunity to be a financial advisor again after being virtually jobless for two years. These are two good Christian men with who share their faith with others around them. I am proud to have been associated with them both.

A multitude of thanks goes to Gary Sacheck, my friend and mentor from Schwab who listened when I needed someone to listen. He is one of the best supervisors that I ever had.

My appreciation goes to my HR person on call, David Meeks whom I have known since my college ΣAE fraternity days. He was there for firm guidance when the going got tough.

Gratitude also goes to my long time friend Aaron Omar who kept me focused on the fact that I am smarter than most anyone else is out there. He told me that success would come for me. All I had to do was keep fighting and telling my story.

If you are a Catholic like me, then I hope that you been enriched by Christ Renews His Parish as I have. If you have not gone through Christ Renews His Parish at your Catholic Church, then sign up. It will change your life forever and help you grow closer to Jesus. With the help of my brothers in Christ, I had the honor and privilege to serve our Christ Renews His Parish team as Lay Director recently. Thanks go to my team of brothers at San Juan Del Rio who helped me through the process and Father John Tetlow for his valuable support.

I especially want to thank Bryan Weiss of Marian Financial Services, Inc. who was also a Lay Director for his Christ Renews His Parish team. He was a great help to me as I prepared to present to the incoming team of men seeking a closer relationship with Jesus. Bryan is a great apostle for Christ.

Further kudos goes to the Attorneys, CPA's, Financial Planners, Financial Advisors, and their Clients who believe in my wise counsel. Without them, I would not be successful.

PREFACE

I began my career in 1984 working in the life insurance business following the example of my father, Hillman E. Johnson. In my first venture in the life insurance business, I affiliated with Southwestern Life Insurance Company as a career agent and soon moved over to work with Hillman and his independent life insurance agency. Several influential people including Frank Deuschle my branch manager, Greg Dunseath, my sales manager and Steve Burk, of Insurance Designers of Kansas City, the smartest person on the planet, all help me get started. I learned from some of the very best, including of course, my dad.

After about four years, I decided to study for the Series 7 and Series 63 licenses, which allowed me to sell securities. My role at the time was to support Hillman in his life insurance agency while at the same time, begin to build a client base of my own.

In 1990, my studies began for the Certified Financial Planner® designation, which consisted of six independent exams. The CFP® program was a two-year program offered by the College for Financial Planning. I successfully passed all six exams in a row, which was no easy feat. The CFP® curriculum is very challenging. You cannot go in there and wing it. After a diligent effort, I earned the coveted CFP® designation in December of 1992.

Mutual funds and variable products were very popular in the early nineties and I wanted to learn more about them for the benefit of my clients. The College for Financial Planning offered a new designation entitled the Chartered Mutual Fund Counselor®. I studied the nine modules and successfully obtained the CMFC® designation.

In 1991, I ventured out and started my own financial planning shop. I studied for and passed the Series 24 exam and later the Series 65 exam. For the next eight years, I was an independent financial planner. My first registered investment adviser firm was my own. I named it Ambitions,

Inc. I was a little ahead of myself back then and had not built Ambitions, Inc. into the asset size it needed to be to survive. It was a great learning experience nevertheless.

In 1999, I had the best year ever up to that point, but knew that the market was going down soon because of the insanity of the tech and internet bubbles.

Early in the year 2000, I made the decision to go to work for Charles Schwab & Co. Inc. as an Investment Specialist. At Charles Schwab, I studied for and passed the Series 9 and Series 10. The Series 9 and 10 licenses allowed me to be a NYSE Branch Office Manager. What this means is, if your firm is a NYSE member, then you are qualified to manage a branch office for them by virtue of passing these two exams.

My wife Natalie works at Allstate Insurance Company as a claims adjuster and has a thirty plus year career going with them. I often kid her about being a dinosaur. She started working for Allstate when she was only eighteen. In the spring of 2002, they announced that they were closing the Little Rock, Arkansas office of Allstate. We reviewed the respective job sites of both Schwab and Allstate and decided to move to Jacksonville, Florida. Natalie was able to transfer with Allstate (in about 5 minutes) and I accepted the Jacksonville Investor Center Manager position with Schwab, which took me about 8 weeks. I had to compete with many good candidates. Gary Sacheck, my branch manager in Little Rock helped me land the position.

While at the Jacksonville Investor Center, I helped turn around the office by making tough personnel decisions and improving client sales and services. They needed a hatchet man and unfortunately, I fit the bill. Letting people go was not something that I enjoyed. We ended up successfully turning the office around with a few bumps along the way. It has been over four years since I left and I believe most everyone that was there when I left is still working there.

After my years at Schwab, I started the firm that I now own, Rick Johnson Family Office LLC. It was after leaving Schwab in late 2004, that I finished writing my first book, *Invest Successfully and Protect Your Assets*. By now, I had also earned the Registered Financial Consultant® designation in 2004.

In 2005, I continued my studies and earned the Chartered Advisor for Senior Living™ through the American College. By now, I held the Series 7, 9, 10, 24, 63 and 65 licenses. In addition, I earned the CASL™, CFP®, CMFC®, and RFC® designations. I also picked up my real estate license along the way.

I spent some time with Allstate Financial, but that did not work out as planned. They have some good people at Allstate and they are a great company. It just did not work out.

Searching for a better opportunity, I moved to SK Advisors LLC, formerly Veritas Wealth Management LLC, which is a registered investment adviser. There are two fantastic advisors who work at SK Advisors, namely Bruce Kelvington and Roger Shealy.

After I left SK Advisors, I went to work for First Financial Education Centers LLC, an insurance agency, and their affiliated registered investment adviser firm, First Financial Advisors LLC.

Today, I work with one other financial advisor whom I have helped in the past. I help him manage his client's assets. In addition, I work with my own select group of clients. Further, I am always looking to add to my client base.

My secret to being a knowledgeable financial planner is very simple. I have a voracious appetite for reading, studying and staying abreast of my industry. I put in the extra effort to study my profession. Over the years, through trial and error, I have learned not to listen to the mainstream. I have discovered the truth with regard to investing successfully. You must have a financial plan and follow a consistent process. It is also very, very important that risk is controlled and kept at reduced levels throughout both bull and bear markets. If you control your risk, then you will have a much better chance at success.

INTRODUCTION

In this book, I will intersperse pieces of my life, my friends, and my family. I will talk about things that you may think having nothing to do with a plan and a process for your success. However, that would be an erroneous assumption on your part. Without a doubt, I will teach you about life, faith, forgiveness, wisdom, and moral values. You will know who I am in the end and you will know that I am someone that you can trust to help you with your life. The experiences in life that I have had are the steps on the spiritual highway to eternal life. Money is not what is important in this world. It is about helping other people in their spiritual journey. At least that is what I believe and that is why I do what I do.

There are many people in my profession who measure their self worth based on the amount of client assets they have under management. I base my self worth on how I unselfishly help others. When your goals as a financial advisor are to make as much money as you can, then your moral values are unbalanced, in my opinion. Instead, the goals of your clients should be primary.

With God's grace, I was born into this world on September 26, 1956 in Little Rock, Arkansas. My father was Billy Joe Allison and my mother, Donna Jean Bridges. Bill and Donna were only married for a short time. He was in the military having served in both the Army and the Air Force. Bill was also a Korean War Veteran. After the military, Bill went into law enforcement. He began his police career in Midland, Texas. Later he moved to California and had three children Jon, Tami, and Kelly. I have had the great opportunity to get to know Jon, Tami, and Kelly. Jon lives in Arroyo Grande, California. Tami lives in Las Vegas and Kelly lives just outside of Orlando.

While Bill was in California, he applied for the Chief of Police position in the Central Coast area of California. He served as the Chief of Police of Arroyo Grande, California. As time passed, he eventually moved back to Arkansas to accept a Chief of Police position in Camden, Arkansas. Camden is in the southern part of the state of Arkansas.

If you have ever wondered why I take a stand on right and wrong, perhaps it is because I have a little bit of law enforcement blood in me. I also majored in Criminal Justice at the University of Arkansas-Little Rock. I visited several prisons in Arkansas and Mississippi, not to mention the Pulaski County Jail during my studies. Studying Criminal Justice gives you a background on both social and psychological issues.

I do not ever recall meeting my father, Bill. My stepsister Tami told me that he came to see me when I was about six years old. I have no memory of that meeting.

I was a senior in high school when he passed away suddenly of arteriosclerosis at the very young age of 39. He was in the hospital and the doctors told him that he was going to have to change his diet and take better care of himself, but later in the day, he died. This happened in 1974. Today, with the advances in medicine, he most certainly would have had a much better chance to survive.

He moved back to Arkansas to have a relationship with me, Tami told me. He was waiting until I turned eighteen, then he figured my mom could not stop him from seeing me. This has given me some comfort over the years. I have no idea of the relationship between my mom and Bill since I only heard one side of the story. My mom just never talked about it to me. I learned about my father Bill from Harold Allison, my aunts Betty and Nancy, my stepsiblings Jon, Tami and Kelly and their mom, Margaret Allison. They were also kind enough to give me some old pictures of my father, Bill Allison when he was young. We had kind of an Unsolved Mysteries moment when we all got together again about ten years ago.

My mom is one of the most generous and thoughtful people that you will ever met. She has made great sacrifices in her life for her family. She will do anything for those she loves. I love her dearly.

My mom went to the famed Central High School in Little Rock, Arkansas that made national news in 1957 for not allowing black students into school. She had already graduated by the time that all that mess had made the national news. During this period, my mom was married to Bill and I was little more than a year old. When I was two years old, they were divorced and my mom had re-married Hillman Eugene Johnson of Sardis, Mississippi. If no one had told me that I had another father, I probably would have never known. Hillman was the dad that I grew up with and the only dad that I knew.

During my early teen years, I spent a lot of time with my maternal grandmother, Bernice Bernadette Bridges. Her maiden name was Morte and her family hailed from Portugal. Most of the Bridges in our family have dark, olive skin. I have no idea what happened to me. My son Marshall inherited the Morte look.

My grandmother was a devout Catholic. She prayed the rosary, attended mass and was close to Monsignor Allen of Holy Souls Catholic Church. I went to public schools from the first through ninth grades, but because of her example of faith, I wanted to be a Catholic. Therefore, when I was 14 years old, I converted to the Catholic religion. My "Granny" as we affectionately called her suffered from kidney disease later in her life, but this did not stop her from going to mass on Sundays. I often would attend mass with her and watch her walk into mass in pain. It was a struggle, but she fought on. She was a shining example of faith, reverence, and perseverance for Christ. She was the kind of inspiration that a teenage boy needs, if you know what I mean.

In my sophomore year of high school, I enrolled in Catholic High School for Boys in Little Rock. Oh, my dear friend, what an honor, and privilege it was to go to this school. The school was full of priests who were my teachers. We had a few lay teachers at the time. I mostly recall the priests as my teachers. The principal of the school was Father George Tribou. Father Tribou was something special and named Arkansas' man of the year several times.

Father Tribou believed in discipline and devotion. Friend, you did not want to get in his doghouse, let me tell you. If you were stupid enough to try to smoke a cigarette at school, then he had a little discipline for you. He would put you and your smoker friends in about a four foot by four-foot closet with a bucket in the middle. Then, he would give everyone big fat cigars to smoke since it was evident to him that these boys liked to smoke. After a few minutes of filling a small space with cigar smoke, suddenly the reason for the bucket became clear. It was to hold their puke. After everyone puked their guts out, then he would let them out. Depending on their attitude when they got out of there, he might feel the need for a little paddling to go with it. Discipline works. It is sad that the principal of high schools cannot institute a similar punishment today.

I can still remember the words Father Tribou spoke to us at our graduation. He had a huge impact on our lives. I attended his funeral and was very proud to have been one of his students. Still to this day, I look back on that time in my life as truly, truly special.

When my father Bill passed away, a priest named Father Gaston Hebert checked me back into Catholic High. He was my English teacher and he was a disciplinarian too. I have never forgotten the words that he spoke to me that day as I checked back into school after Bill's funeral. He said, "Did you know him?" I replied, "No". It has always been a black hole in my life not knowing my real Father, but I had to accept the circumstances as they were and move forward.

Hillman and my mom ended up having three more kids, Shari Ann, David Hillman, and Gary Dennis Johnson. My sister was born six years after me, David seven years later and Gary, nine years later. Shari is very smart. She graduated Summa Cum Laude from Hendrix University in Conway, Arkansas. That was her graduate studies. She loves to run, also. She can run for miles and miles without a problem. Of course, she does not have an ounce of fat on her as a result. She has three boys, Jake, Jared, and Jensen. Shari is married to Joe Thielke who is very successful at anything he does. Joe is well connected and entrenched in the Conway community.

David spent a lot of his time working for Coca-Cola, and then he worked for the local beer distributorship. He was a delivery driver for both companies. Anytime there was a boxing match or a bachelor party, it was at Dave's place. He has one daughter named Natalie who is a gorgeous young woman today. She recently sent us a letter telling us about her life. She is twenty-two now and has a job as a 911 dispatcher. Her boyfriend, Dwayne is currently in Afghanistan working as a helicopter gunner. He is due home in January of 2009. Please say a prayer for him and give him thanks for his service to our country if you know or ever meet him.

Gary worked for my dad for a long time, and then spent some time with Cingular Wireless. The last few years, he went into the home building business and has experienced a very rough time as you can imagine. He and his builder friend Rodney built some awesome homes, though. The quality is just outstanding. He has two sons, Cameron and Colin. Gary will rebound, recover, and move forward. I am sure of it. He has what it takes to be successful.

When we were young, we all lived in an area of Little Rock known as Meadowcliff. Up until the time when Gary was born, we all lived in a 1,000 square foot house. My dad was six foot five and drove a VW Beetle. That was an original VW Beetle by the way. He spent time as a dance instructor for Arthur Murray studios, before he moved on to be an insurance agent for Southwestern Life Insurance Company of Dallas, Texas.

Hillman had many gifts. He was a character. Everyone wanted to be his friend even if you just met him. He had a habit of giving people nicknames. The bad people of the insurance industry, he would call Jesse James. In fact, I remember a couple of brothers in the insurance business he used to call Frank and Jesse James. He would call his lawyer friends Loophole. Of course, you know who the last person to let you down was. It was the undertaker, he would say. You could not be his friend without having a nickname. That was the way it was. I did not escape the nickname tag either. He used to call me "Hollywood" because of my propensity to wear cool sunglasses.

Hillman was an avid hunter. He hunted deer, turkey, doves, ducks, geese, pheasants, elk, mule deer, and squirrels. Hillman used to joke with his friends with a bullet in his pocket. The joke was he was ready to go hunting and he only needed one bullet since he was a crack shot. I learned a lot about hunting, camping and fishing from my dad Hillman. Both my brothers, David and Gary took to hunting more than I hunted, but there is something special about going out in the woods and getting away from the rat race. I always enjoyed it regardless.

When I was young, I became a baseball player. I love baseball and always have. My career spanned from the age of nine until the age of 15. When I turned sixteen, I wanted a car, so I got a job. Baseball was over, at least for the time being. I was good at baseball though. Later, I will give you a neat baseball story that you find truly amazing.

I worked at St. Vincent's Hospital, a Catholic hospital by the way, in Little Rock. My meager salary at the time was not a salary at all, but was an hourly wage of $1.65 an hour. I was able to save up $1,000 and buy my first car by working nights and weekends. My first car was a 1968 pea green Ford Mustang. It was probably the ugliest color green that you have ever seen, but it was all mine and I was very proud of it. I bought my own cars from that point on. My parents never bought me a car. They helped me get financing, but I always paid for my own cars.

When I was eighteen, I moved out of the family home and got an apartment. I never went back after that. Back then, we had roommates to help pay the rent. One of my roommates was Mike Rowland, my scrawny little friend from Catholic High. Both of us weighed about 145 pounds all soaking wet. I wish that were the case today. We met in the gym at Catholic High. Mike was shooting free throws. He could stand there, shoot 100 free throws, and probably make 90% of them. Not me, I was lucky if I could hit the rim. Mike grew up in North Little Rock. He also came from a family of four kids like me. He had a brother, Charlie and two sisters, Patty and Kelly.

Mike and I joined the same fraternity at the University of Arkansas at Little Rock, Sigma Alpha Epsilon. In 1975, Mike and I went to Evanston Illinois to attend the ΣAE Leadership School there on the campus of Northwestern University. Mike and I had a blast on Rush Street in Chicago hanging out with fellow ΣAE's from across the nation. We learned a lot about the history of our fraternity that week. We learned how to be leaders in society too. I must have learned something, because I became the President of ΣAE for the Arkansas Beta chapter.

It was here that I learned how to handle a budget and turn things around. When I took office as ΣAE President, I inherited a deficit of over $1,000. As the ΣAE President, I made a few changes like charging for events that used to be free and I ended up leaving office with over $1,000 in the bank. I enjoyed the challenges of being in charge and turning things around. This was really my first experience as a financial advisor.

While in college, we watched as Mike Rowland's dad passed away of emphysema. We all knew it was coming. Mr. Rowland was a funny person. I can remember going over to his house and him being on an oxygen machine. He used to joke about being on the "drunk-o-meter". Mike and I had something in common. We both lost our fathers at young ages. We ended up rooming together in an apartment. He had the Stevie Wonder album and I had the record player. Mike and I both worked in the restaurant business. He was a waiter and I worked in the bar as a busboy and bar back.

Sometimes, you have a defining moment in your life and you have to be able to recognize it for what it is. One day, Mike overslept and missed the morning mass. This was not something that Mike ever did. He did not miss mass. I can still remember the look on his face when he realized that he missed mass. This was a message for me from Christ. Still to this day, anytime that I even think about not going to mass, I ask myself, "Would Mike have missed mass today?" I know the answer. He ended up going to the afternoon mass that day. I have never forgotten that experience.

I can remember going over to Mike's house and his little sister Kelly holding my arm. She was blind from Juvenile Diabetes. Kelly would hold my arm as we walked around the house. Mike would be busy looking for something or talking with his mom. Kelly and I would just talk and talk. She was the sweetest thing and an inspiration for all blind young people. She attended the Arkansas School for the Deaf and Blind in Little Rock. Tragically, one horrible day two young men kidnapped, raped, and murdered her. It was just the most tragic thing to happen. How could anyone kill such a sweet girl who was blind no less and indefensible?

Little did we realize that at the time, the prosecutor was involved in drugs. Of course, he made a deal with the devil and botched the trial. These young men got away with murder. It was the outrage of the community. Mike took it hard. It was a very tough period for the Rowland family.

One of the best examples of faith in Christ and more importantly forgiveness that I witnessed was the reaction of Mrs. Rowland at her daughter's funeral. In front of everyone, she knelt beside her daughter's casket and prayed to God to forgive the men that murdered her daughter. Mrs. Rowland sensed the outrage in the church and wanted to teach us all what it meant to be a follower of Christ Jesus. You have to forgive even in the most unforgiveable circumstances. I have never forgotten this day. Again, God was talking to me through her example.

I met my wife Natalie at a place called, The Wrangler. It was a hybrid country western and disco bar. Keep in mind this was in the eighties. She was actually on a date with another person, but she knew one of my friend's little brother. Therefore, I just asked my friend's little brother who she was. I found out that she worked for Allstate Insurance and worked part time at M.M. Cohn's, a local department store. I fell for her right at that moment. I had to meet her and ask her out. Somehow, I garnered the courage to walk into her Allstate office, sit down in front of her, and ask her out. She said yes to my delight.

We were married on October 22, 1988. Not long after that, we were expecting our first child. I was 32 at the time and she was 30. We were like everyone else in America. We thought we would have two or three kids, live in a nice house and have a great life together. Everything would go as planned.

As Catholics, you cannot just go get married. You have to go see the good Father. In our case, it was Father Hebert, my disciplinarian English teacher from Catholic High. He gave us a test for compatibility. He mentioned to us that we had scored the highest that he had ever seen on this test. That did not surprise Natalie or me. We knew we were soul mates.

Our first son Reese Cannon Johnson was born on Labor Day in 1989. Natalie had a Reese's Peanut Butter Cup wrapper tacked to the wall to help her with her focal point. You know when your wife reads those baby books, and then you find out all kinds of things. Now I knew what a focal point was.

Natalie was in labor for what seemed like an eternity. Finally, the doctor said the words I wanted to hear, "C-Section". I was bushed and ready to get this birth going. That is just like a man, isn't it? My wife was doing all the work, not me.

Reese was born and he was having a little trouble breathing. I did not quite understand all this doctor stuff. The doctor who delivered him was gone and the pediatrician was not working on Labor Day. Reese was placed under an oxygen tent in the Neonatal ICU. There was no doctor to be found anywhere on that Labor Day. I literally did not know whether my son was going to live or die. Finally, I begged a nurse to call a doctor and let me speak with him. Natalie was out of it and completely unaware of what was happening. The doctor on call, told me not to worry. He said this was standard protocol. It certainly did not feel routine to me.

It was five days later and Reese was still in the Neonatal ICU unit. We had not seen hide nor hair of the pediatrician. Finally, he burst through the door of Natalie's hospital room and said that we could take him home. I stopped him and said, "Wait just a minute. He has been in an oxygen tent all week and now he can just go?" Something seemed screwy to me about this. His chest was sinking in when he took a breath. It just did not seem right to me. This doctor uttered the infamous words that I have never forgotten, "treat him like a normal baby".

In December of 1989, I was working for my dad Hillman and we won a trip to Hong Kong. We left Reese who was now three months old in capable hands with Natalie's mother. During the day while she worked, she took Reese to the home of a couple who had taken care of my brother David's daughter as a child. Although we did not want to leave our son at the age of three months and go off to Hong Kong, we decided it would be okay. Natalie and I had an eerie feeling as if we would be killed in a plane crash.

Little did we realize that it was not us, but Reese who was going to die. Reese died suddenly of Sudden Infant Death Syndrome while we were in Hong Kong. I did not have any idea about SIDS. I learned quickly however by spending several hours in the medical school library.

Hong Kong is thirty long hours away. All I could think about was getting back to see my son. I wanted to see him one last time. God comforted us on that long flight back. We had time to prepare. At the funeral parlor, I knelt down by my son's casket and kissed him on the forehead. It gave me peace and comfort. I was close to the Lord. A couple of weeks before, we had baptized Reese into the Catholic faith. On that same day, Natalie and I had renewed our vows. Natalie gave me a crucifix on a necklace that day which is very special to me since I received it on the day Reese was baptized. The priest who performed these memorable ceremonies for us was Father Gaston Hebert.

Losing a child is one of the most difficult things that any parent can endure. You do not ever get over it. Natalie and I chose to channel our grief to help others. We joined the local Compassionate Friends group, that later become the Bereaved Parents group. We ended up running the group for a while. Let me tell you, when you are around people who have all lost their children, life takes on a different perspective. You quit feeling sorry for yourself and start thinking about other people.

Later after Reese died, we decided to try again for another child. We were blessed with the birth of our son Marshall. Marshall was on one of those machines that monitors your breathing, because of what happened to Reese. He set it off 28 times in the first 30 days. We were scared to death that Marshall may have the same fate as Reese. Somehow, with God's grace Marshall managed to make it. Marshall is an unbelievable gift. He is truly a remarkable young man. As of this writing, he is in Advance Placement classes in his senior year in high school. They just had senior skip day at his school, but Marshall went to school. He did not skip school. It was his decision. Marshall told Natalie, "I hope you guys realize what a good kid you have". We certainly do Marshall. You are one of God's greatest gifts to us. He makes me very proud as a father.

Soon after Marshall was born, we decided to have another child. As is the case with most people, we assumed that we could easily have another child. Why would we think differently? Unfortunately, we had a miscarriage. Not being the kind to give up very easily, we tried again. Then, we had a second miscarriage. This was very disheartening. After having lost Reese and being Catholic, to us, we were losing children. It was not just a miscarriage.

One of these miscarriages, I can't remember which one it was, but I woke up in the middle of the night to find my wife passed out on the bathroom floor. She had fainted and hit her head. It scared the living daylights out of me, but she ended up being okay.

We tried again for another child, but to our dismay, we had yet a third miscarriage. I was almost forty now and thought perhaps Marshall was it for us. We prayed for another child.

After our third miscarriage, Natalie and I sat down one evening and watched a little movie called, "Rudy". It was about a Catholic kid nicknamed Rudy whose dream it was to go to Notre Dame. This man named Rudy never gave up. He achieved his dream under adverse circumstances and endured numerous setbacks along the way. He wanted to give up, but he persevered in the midst of great despair. Natalie and I just looked at each other and said that we had to keep trying.

Natalie got excited after watching this movie and said if we have a boy, we are going to name it R-U-D-Y and if we have a girl, then we will name her R-U-D-I. We had a girl and we named her Rudi Michelle Johnson. She has red hair like her mother. Miss Rudi is a little pistol according to my wife. Marshall was great about school and homework. Rudi lives to play everyday and school is secondary. Somehow, she ends up making good grades, but I believe she could be straight A's if she tried a little harder.

Rudi is my sweet pumpkin love. She likes me to tuck her at night. It is not every night mind you, but quite often. I kiss her on the forehead, tell her goodnight and tell her that I love her. I hope that you do the same to your children.

As we move forward through this book together, I will mix in some more personal stories for you. I believe that it is important for you to know the real person that is Rick Johnson.

EXPERIENCE IS A GREAT TEACHER

A little over twenty years ago, I was just like some of you. I did not know how to invest money successfully. I also knew that if I ever was going to be successful investing other people's money, then I needed to make a commitment to studying my profession. Education never ceases, in my opinion. You should always strive to improve your education level as long as you live. This is my approach to life.

I am going to be open and honest with you about who I am and my experiences in this industry. It is a very tough business, as you will see in my story below. In return, you can expect me to zero in on costly mistakes that you or your financial professional may have made with regard to your investments. I will hold nothing back. Some people may interpret my story as a negative. For me, it is the fabric of who I am. A little insight into what goes on behind the scenes may benefit you. Regardless, I am proud of the journey that I have taken.

In 1984, I entered the business as an insurance agent working with my dad, Hillman Eugene Johnson and his independent life insurance agency. He was as they say in the business, a heavy hitter. I learned a lot from him and I dearly miss his eternally optimistic, tell it like it is attitude. My dad was something special. His circle of friends was unbelievable. He was six foot five inches tall. Hillman Johnson was a legend. Ask anyone who knew him.

By 1988, I had gravitated to the securities business and earned my Series 7. Insurance agents back then only sought the Series 6 license that does not allow you to sell stocks and bonds. At the time, I thought to myself, "Why should I limit myself like that?" As a result, I went for the Series 7 instead.

Natalie was pregnant with Reese when I passed the Series 7.

After about six years in the business, I decided to begin studying for the Certified Financial Planner designation offered through the College of Financial Planning. After Reese died, I began my CFP® studies. There were six individual courses required to obtain the CFP® mark. I can still remember the sacrifice on my family, not to mention the toll it took on me. Marshall was born in November of 1990. I can remember sitting at the kitchen table around midnight holding Marshall in my arms while studying for the CFP® designation. It was well worth it however, because in 1992, I earned the CFP® designation. This was a great personal accomplishment for me.

In December of 1993, we were all over at my sister's house celebrating her first son's first birthday. The whole family was there that evening. My brother David had been deer hunting all day down in South Arkansas and he was somewhat tired. He asked my Mom and Dad to take his daughter, "Little Natalie" home with them and he would come get her the next morning. This turned out to be a special blessing, because on the way home that night, my brother was killed in an accident with an 18-wheeler. It could have been him *and* his daughter who were killed. He saved his daughter's life that night by doing what he did. I miss my brother deeply. He and I lived on the same street in Little Rock at the time. His nickname was Diamond Dave.

My dad took David dying hard. This was his first son. Dad was bad about going to the doctor. He was six foot five and weighed about two hundred ninety pounds, but was scared to go to the doctor. You would think that someone that big would not be scared of anything. He had a couple of nicknames himself. Some of his friends called him "Wolf" and others called him "290" in reference to his weight.

My dad and I had a good thing going back then. He was the life insurance person and I was the securities person. However, after I received my CFP® designation, I yearned to strike out on my own. I soon learned that I would need a Series 24 license to do this. Therefore, in 1991, in between studying for my CFP® courses, I earned the Series 24. This test gave me the privilege of being a registered principal and branch office manager for an independent broker/dealer. It allowed me to hire and supervise other Series 6, or Series 7 representatives. At one time, I had five other representatives working for me. They were all from the insurance industry.

Three years after David died; Dad was having some health problems. He finally went to the doctor and we found out that he had liver cancer. We were all devastated. Even to this day, we never really saw him drink much, just a few beers here and there. Perhaps he was just one of those people whose body could not take much alcohol. I know people who drink like a fish and I am sure that you do too. Nothing ever happens to them.

One weekend, my Dad and I had planned to meet in Orlando to go see the NASCAR Café at Universal Studios. He was a big NASCAR fan and had been to several races. We were at work that Friday and in walked Father Hebert. I was working with my Dad at his office at this time to help. My mom was also there and I asked her what Father Hebert was doing in the back with Dad. She told me that he wanted to convert to the Catholic religion and accept Jesus Christ as his Lord and Savior, because of my example. She said he was impressed by the example that I led by attending mass with my family. Believe me, I am no saint. However, it is an amazing thing when a Father follows a son to Christ. I am thankful to have had a small part in his conversion.

That weekend, I headed down to Tampa, Florida. I had plans to meet my Dad in Orlando. As I was almost to Tampa, I received a call from one of my fraternity brothers that my friend Mike Rowland had died. I could not believe it was true. A crack addict who waited for him as he came out of his drapery business one night murdered him. I stayed in Tampa that night, turned right around the next day, and headed back to Little Rock for Mike's funeral. On the way back, I received some calls that my Dad was in the hospital. Then, the calls stopped. Therefore, I called and found out that he passed away, too.

God had protected Natalie and me when Reese died. We were blessed in the fact that we did not find Reese not breathing and unresponsive ourselves. God was at work again here by having me out of town when Mike and my Dad died. He knows that it was better for me to not watch either of them pass away. Both Mike and my Dad spent a little time in the hospital right before they died. Mike was temporarily on life support, but he was already gone. My Dad did have some family and friends with him when he passed.

There were two funerals that week. Mike's was first. As I recall, there were seven priests at Mike's funeral. If you are Catholic, have you ever seen seven priests at someone's funeral? That tells you the respect and devotion that Mike Rowland had earned in his 39 years on earth. As Natalie and I were leaving, Father Hebert came up to us crying asking me why I was at Mike's funeral. He was my friend I told him.

Father Hebert did my Dad's funeral two days later. I had a moment to sit with my Dad while his casket was open. I looked at him and saw his face with no pain. He was happy, I thought because he had committed to Christ on his last weekend of life. He had pushed the envelope his whole life, but came home to Christ when it mattered. Sitting there that day, just him and me, I felt as if he was telling me and Christ was telling me that he made it. His soul was indeed in Heaven.

Perhaps, you can come to Christ long before your last weekend. The Lord will accept you. Seek and you will find.

By 1997, I began studying for the Chartered Mutual Fund Counselor designation that was also from the College of Financial Planning. This designation focused primarily on mutual funds and variable products.

By this time, I had earned the respect of others as being very knowledgeable about investing and financial planning. The bull market was nearing its peak by early 2000 and I knew that it was going to come down and come down hard. My crystal ball clearly told me to move to a good firm and I chose Charles Schwab & Co., Inc.

Yes folks, it is true. I started with Schwab at the peak of the bull market in March of 2000. Schwab made the mistake that many investors did in 1999 and 2000 by believing that they were never going to see another poor day again. They made purchases like everyone else that they should not have. They hired too many employees. In addition, they opened a new service center that they should not have.

This was really my first experience as an employee with corporate America. The whole time I was there, they were closing offices and terminating employees. Through it all, we had to produce sales. The meaning of sales at Schwab was to bring in new assets.

Schwab is an amazing company. Mr. Schwab himself is one of the great visionaries of our country. This company had the uncanny ability to attract new assets from its existing client base. While I was in Little Rock, I averaged over 11.7 million dollars in new assets a quarter for the two years that I was there. Our team of David Barnett, Dragi Misic, Rob Tiffee and our leader Gary Sacheck achieved Chairman's Club, which was a top honor for us at Schwab. This is no small feat let me tell you.

I made it a point to go by and see Mike Rowland's Mom every now and then. Most people send their condolences at the time of the funeral, and then they slide off into oblivion. They do this because they do not know what to say. It was different with me. Mike Rowland would kick my butt if I did not go see his Mom.

On one occasion, Mike's Mom told me about his generous heart. She said that right before he died, he heard of an elderly woman who was sleeping on her couch, because she did not have a bed. Mike would have none of that mind you. He loaded up his own bed, took it over to the elderly woman's house, and gave it to her. Would you think to do that? Mike was an amazing person and I was blessed to have him as my friend. We all need friends like that.

After my first two years at Schwab, I accepted the Branch Manager position in Jacksonville, Florida. It was here that I learned the most about corporate America and the investing public.

When I first arrived in Jacksonville, I found myself in a very tough situation. It was a turn around situation. Somehow, I had to find a way to attract new employees who wanted to work and ring the cash register at the same time. The first quarter I was there, we earned a bonus. It was the first time in over a year and a half that the office had earned a bonus. I continued that success and built on it.

During my tenure in Jacksonville, I absorbed two other branch offices that were closed. Therefore, I had to deal with people in West Jacksonville, Gainesville and Tallahassee who were mad that Schwab had closed their branch. The Tallahassee branch had experienced a situation where all the employees walked out the door one day and went to work for a competing firm. I went from having a cozy little Jacksonville branch to one of the largest geographical branches in the nation. Oh, they gave me South Georgia, too.

All the while, I still had to hit my sales target, which by the way had increased 400% year over year. A rep in my office had to bring in $3,800,000 in net new assets per quarter in 2003. In 2004, they had to bring in $16,000,000 in a quarter. Welcome to corporate America. Insane as this was, we got very aggressive and we did it. Thanks in large part to the team that I had put together in Jacksonville.

One of the people that I hired, Teb Yu is just an outstanding financial professional. He and I enjoyed working together to bring in the big numbers. He was motivated to be successful and liked achieving goals. Not only did he achieve them, but also typically, each quarter, he would be the new asset leader in the office. It turned out that he was the top Schwab Investment Specialist in the State of Florida for 2004. He is currently driving around in a black on black Corvette and he recently purchased a new house, so he must be doing okay. Without Teb, we could not have been as successful as we were at Schwab. Of course, we were a team, everyone contributed, but Teb and I enjoyed working together immensely.

I am jazzed up about achieving success and this latest goal from my supervisor was a challenge that I enjoyed. In the quarter that I left, the Jacksonville Branch had the best quarter in its history. They did over $80,000,000 in one quarter! When I walked out the door, six weeks into the quarter, they had $57,000,000 in the house. My first quarter we did $8,000,000 and my last quarter we did $80,000,000. I wonder, do you think I may have a little talent? Make no mistake that I went out on top!

A funny thing happens when a company has a brain drain of talent. They are left with the people who are more successful at circling their own wagons, rather than those who are good for the company. In the four years and three months that I was employed there, I went through seven Regional Vice Presidents. Seven! One poor guy only lasted one month. Since I have resigned, I have heard three more RVP's have been terminated, or excuse me, I meant retired on their own terms. Isn't it funny how if you are a rank and file employee you are laid off and if you are an executive you found that it was time to retire?

Right before I resigned, I spoke with a Schwab client who was a 41-year veteran of General Electric and filled him in a little bit on the management and employee shuffle going on at Schwab. He listened to me and said, "That's bad management". I knew he was right. This person worked alongside Jack Welch. "There should not be that kind of turnover in the RVP position," he told me.

I like working with people who believe that you can achieve great things. Why would you believe anything else? As a supervisor, you build people up even if it means that they take your job, or move up the ladder and get a job better than yours. That is how you manage people. You sacrifice your ego and self-esteem to help others achieve greatness.

Ask any senior Human Resources Manager who performs exit interviews with corporate employees and they will tell you there is one major reason people leave corporations. That reason is they did not get along with their supervisor. When it comes down to it, I suppose that I am just like most people who leave corporate America. I just did not want to take it anymore.

One thing about me is that I am not a "yes man". I will stand up for what is right even if it means sacrificing my job. Having had the time to reflect on it all again, my Christian values were in conflict. The senior executives at Schwab, very shortly after I resigned, I might add, came to the same conclusion that I did. There was something fishy going on in that regional office. They ended up firing my ex-boss and her boss, too. If only they would have picked up the phone to hear my side of the story, maybe things would have been different.

What kind of individual would walk away from a job like this? Granted it takes a lot of courage to put yourself in a tenuous financial position by walking away, but what kind of person would you be if you did not stand up for what you believed. I have no interest in being affiliated with unethical, selfish people. I recently walked away from another firm for similar reasons. I want nothing to do with unethical people.

My faith tells me that this is what was supposed to happen in my life. I have moved on to greater things. It is true what they say…what goes around comes around.

I was saddened to read about a high-ranking executive who recently left a major company. In the article about his departure, they described him as a little too independent and ambitious. Oh, how sad it is to see that kind of corporate mentality. You want people who are independent thinkers and ambitious in corporate America. They are the ones who make America great! If your corporate leadership is filled with people good at picking off the independent thinkers and replacing them with "yes" men, then you have a fragile empire in my opinion.

Like this chapter title says, experience is a great teacher. Nevertheless, the amazing thing is that I still love this business and I still love working with Charles Schwab & Co. I still work with Schwab everyday. Instead of being on the retail side of Charles Schwab, now I am on the institutional side of Charles Schwab. My firm maintains our client's accounts at Schwab Institutional. This works out well for me, because I know Schwab inside and out.

I am not in this career to build personal wealth at the sacrifice of my clients. Instead, I would rather do what is best for my clients. When you take the "me" out of the equation, then you see it is an easy decision. The sooner you learn that helping others is more important than helping yourself, it is at that juncture you will find that your life has new meaning.

My present firm has some talented people. More important than talent is the fact they are Christian people who have high ethical standards and strong moral values. These things are more aligned with who I am as a person. God always has a plan for you and me. You just have to believe. Read Jeremiah 29:11 for inspiration and proof that even Jesus has a plan for you. I have Jeremiah 29:11 as a refrigerator magnet and I look at it often. God is just using me as the instrument to deliver your plan to you. Believe me, once you make that commitment to the Lord, then he takes care of you.

Since, my first book, I have earned the Chartered Advisor for Senior Living designation. If you look into the future, you will see that the baby boomers are getting older. Many baby boomers will have to face new life changing issues. The CASL™ designation gives me an added edge with a deeper understanding of the baby boomers. I was awarded the Registered Financial Consultant (RFC®) designation a few years ago. This requires 40 hours of continuing education each year to maintain. There will be even more studying for me in the future.

Lest we not forget that, I have completed my 16th year as a Certified Financial Planner, too. I spend 30 hours a year in continuing education for that license.

Financial Planning

Real financial planners hold a professional designation such as the CFP®. Fake financial planners are insurance agents from out of town. I am just kidding all you insurance guys and gals. That is an old joke my Dad, Hillman used to say.

There are professional standards that we real financial planners live by. Chief among them is to put our client's interests before our own. The process and the plan go together. You want to understand the processes involved with your financial planner.

CFP's typically follow a six-step process with clients. This process is the following:

1. Establishing and Defining the Relationship with our Client
2. Gathering Client Data
3. Analyzing and Evaluating the Client's Financial Status
4. Developing and Presenting the Financial Planning Recommendations
5. Implementing the Financial Planning Recommendations
6. Monitoring Responsibilities

Number one (1) means that we will disclosure our background and fees in advance of our relationship. In other words, we are laying it all out there for everyone to see.

Number two (2) means that we need to see everything you have with regards to investments, insurance, budgets, retirement plans, stock options, debt and most anything else financial related. How do you think we can do our job if we do not know everything about you?

Number three (3) means we do our number crunching. We have some cool tools to do this, too. This step takes a lot of time, so be patient.

Number four (4) means that we are ready to meet with you and present our masterpiece to you. The masterpiece is the financial plan, silly.

Number five (5) means that you need to put the financial plan in place. If you do business with a no conflict of interest financial planner who follows my business model, then you will be better off.

Number six (6) means that both you and I have responsibilities in this matter. You have to participate in your own financial plan and notify your financial planner of any changes in your life. The financial planner will monitor your progress and report to you. They still need you to be involved though.

One thing that I can assure you is that you would be a whole lot better off with a living breathing financial plan than without one. Most people go through life making decisions at various times that have no cohesive effort to them. Therefore, the overall achievement of their goals and objectives becomes suspect as a result. You hear a lot about financial plans these days, so I wanted to break it down for you in modules so you can see for yourself.

THE AREAS ENCOMPASSING FINANCIAL PLANNING

There are several primary areas of financial planning. They are the following:

- Liability Planning
- Retirement Planning
- Retirement Income Planning
- Tax Planning
- Long Term Care Planning
- Disability Planning
- Estate Planning
- Investment Planning
- Real Estate Planning

I will describe for you the challenges that are inherent in each of these planning areas. In addition, I will point out the typical mistakes. Finally, I will provide you with concrete solutions that you can implement on your own, or arm you with the information you need to choose a competent financial planner. The financial planner that you choose should be a registered investment adviser and one who does Comprehensive Financial Planning in most if not all of the above areas.

Your Values are Important

One more thing that I would like for you to think about is aligning your financial plan with your values. There has been a lot of talk about values lately, so let me explain with a couple of examples.

Let us assume that there are two individuals and the first individual has as his top values: work, family and health. The second individual has the same values, but in a different order. They are family, health and work.

The first individual who puts work first, family second and health third is most likely a workaholic who neglects his family and his health. This person probably does not have a lot of time for friends, either. If you think this person is going to be committed to a financial plan for the rest of their life, then you are dreaming.

The second individual on the other hand puts their values in this order: family first, health second and work third. This person would have a strong sense of family and would enjoy family activities above all else. Secondarily, they would take care of themselves by eating right and exercising. Work is a distant third on their list. A financial plan would be very appealing to this type of individual, because they have their values in the right place. They would do it for their family.

Now this begs the question, if you are more like the second individual, then are you really going to get along someone like the first individual? Neither, am I. This is why I only want to talk to people who have their values aligned with what is most important to them and that first value is their family. Now you have my reason for being a financial planner and my firm name of Rick Johnson Family Office LLC.

My Goals for You

One of the interesting aspects of working at Schwab was that I helped to a ton of investors. We talked to fifty or more investors every week. As a result, I saw an abundance of investment portfolios and their inherent mistakes. Most of the time, it was not the investor's mistakes. It was the mistakes made by other financial service professionals. These professionals (and I use that term very loosely here) were either in the business of hoping the market turned around, or were out and out inexperienced. Of course, some investors made their own mistakes, too.

Now hear this: If your investment portfolio lost 30% or more in 2008, then it is not properly invested today. Do you get that? If it were invested properly or more defensively, then it would not have lost 30% or more. So, do not sit there stuck in the mud up to your hubcaps and think you will wait until the sun comes out. Make a change!

The goal of this book is to help you understand what a financial plan really is and how you can avoid costly mistakes with your investment portfolio. In addition, I will make you think about ways to align your values with your portfolio. You could probably infer that I am not the kind of person who can work with people that do not have good moral values. Sometimes, I tick off my friends when I see them do things that I do not agree with. I let them know it and generally, they do not like it. Nevertheless, I tell them "how the cow ate the cabbage" which is another way of telling someone the truth.

When your values are in conflict, then this makes you unhappy. We all need to align our values with what we believe in. This will get you on the right track. I believe in helping people be more successful, not only in regards to investing, but also in life.

Value alignment or re-alignment works with your investment portfolio also. If things are out of line with what is important to you, then you will not be happy with the results. My job is to point out ways to make your investment portfolio work in a manner that is aligned with your values.

We are going to cover all the options inside. You may find some things that you are familiar with and others that you are not. Overall, you will find a handy reference for properly designing your investment portfolio and unique thoughts related to financial planning.

As you delve inside, you will find me describing the Challenges, Mistakes and Solutions of the different areas of financial planning. When you refer back to the book, look for the sections entitled Challenges, Mistakes and Solutions for your particular area of interest. For example, if you wanted to find Solutions for Estate Taxes, then you would look at the Solutions section of the Estate Planning chapter.

INVESTOR TYPES

Most investors fall into one of a few categories. Some studies say there are seven or eight distinctive types of investors and other say there are three or four. Personally, I like to keep it simple. Consequentially for purposes of this book, I will only refer to three types of investors.

Some people live busy lives and have plenty of things to worry about. They would rather rely on someone else's counsel for their investment portfolio. I like to call these folks *passive.*

Other people have a little more time on their hands and do not mind doing a little bit on their own. Nevertheless, they would not mind a little affirmation every now and then. I call these people *validators*.

Then, there are the investors who really do not need anyone's help. They like to do things themselves. I call these people *do-it-yourselfers*.

In this book, you will find things that make a whole lot of sense to you. It does not matter whether you are passive investor, a validator type investor, or a do-it-yourself investor. My goal is to help you achieve a better life for you and your family. This is my wish for you, pure and simple.

Investors and financial advisors can use this book as a reference to guide and remind you of what not to do in the future. In addition, it will steer you on a path that you probably have not thought of. That is a path where you achieve your goals and dreams.

FINANCIAL SERVICES
BUSINESS MODELS

I hope that I am not standing in quicksand. Do not think that Certified Financial Planners are just investment professionals. This is far from reality. Instead of investment advice only, we CFP's also do Tax Planning, Retirement Distribution Planning, Estate Planning, Liability Management, Real Estate Planning, Long Term Care Planning, Disability Planning and Retirement Planning.

You can now demand the other services that I described above, sometimes called Comprehensive Financial Planning. I just recently read an inside story of anonymous financial advisors who are faced with laying people off, cutting their own pay, and reducing expenses because they didn't get their clients out of the market. They too lost significant revenue when the overall portfolio of all their clients declined by 30% or more. As a result, they lost 30% or more in revenue. They were crying in their beer let me tell you. They all made the mistakes of only selling investment advice that as we all know is a commodity.

This is my point. People will not continue to pay only for investment advice when they just went through one of toughest bear markets since the Great Depression. Their thinking has changed. Everything is scrutinized now, especially fees as well as the value people receive for their fees. Because of the recent New York person scandal and other scandals that have popped up lately, financial advisors will be put in the unenviable position of having to prove their expertise and now their trustworthiness. The problem with being in the financial advisor field is that it is built on trust. If the trust breakdowns, then that hurts everyone in the business.

Let us examine what you should demand as a potential investment adviser client. First, you should demand full and complete disclosure of all conflicts of interest. You want to do business with a registered investment adviser firm. Do not do business with banks or brokerage firms. Registered investment adviser's have a fiduciary liability to do what is in your best interests. Banks and brokerage firms do not. Let me repeat that. Banks and brokerage firms do not.

Secondarily, you should be able to verify the background of the people that you are considering to hire as a financial advisor. There are independent firms like The National Ethics Bureau who do a seven year background check for looking for any issues with regard to criminal activity, civil lawsuits, license infractions, complaints against designations and several other areas. It would behoove you to see if your advisor is a member of the National Ethics Bureau. Their Web site is www.ethicscheck.com.

Third, you should understand where your investments would be custodied. My suggestion would be to use a financial advisor that uses Charles Schwab & Co. Inc. to hold their client assets. Schwab is the biggest and the best in my opinion. Do not use firms that you have never heard of before like, New York Person Investment Securities, LLC. The total breakdown in this firm was that they were holding the assets, doing the trades and doing the statements. In my firm's case, Schwab holds the assets, my firm does the trades and both Schwab and my firm provide statements that can be compared against each other for verification.

Lastly, you should demand Comprehensive Financial Planning where you get the most bangs for you buck from a registered investment adviser whose principal is a Certified Financial Planner® with years of experience. Yes, you can go to a registered investment adviser whose principal is not a CFP®, but this is kind of like going to an express tax service instead of a more knowledgeable CPA.

Most firms and investment advisors did not perform very well during 2000, 2001 and 2002. There was no place to hide in the later part of 2008 either. The ones who were in value, instead of sticking to growth did better than most. Once again, I have been proven correct that having a large portion of your money in the stock market is foolish.

We are definitely in for more historical stock market returns for sometime. Your expectations for investment returns on your assets should be lower. Forget about making 10% a year. It ain't happening. (Forgive the Arkansas slang. Go Hogs Go!)

If you are an investment advisor, then you had better be offering more than just investment advice.

Customers are getting harder and harder to get, but also to keep. This trend will continue. I have seen this before in the early 80's with insurance companies. When Universal Life came out in the early 80's it was touted as "double your insurance for the same premium that you are paying into that whole life policy". Insurance companies jacked up the commissions to these policies to attract the best sales people. The end result was that the insurance companies cannibalized each other's business. Insurance companies with weak distribution channels were either bought out, or went out of business.

Guess what? The same thing is going on right now in the investment business. Merrill Lynch, Wachovia, AG Edwards have all been gobbled up. Everybody is cannibalizing each other's business. Investment firms are scrambling to bring in business. Employees are being canned by the thousands and will continue to do so, if they do not produce sales results. Companies with strong sales forces will survive. Those without strong sales forces will perish.

Of course, having a little extra cash on the balance sheet would be nice, too. Look at what is happening to General Motors and Chrysler. (Just go to Chapter 11 and get on with it!) Cash is king and so is smart management of assets.

What is the future? I just told you. Weren't you listening? Just kidding! Lighten up, will you?

There is a new business model for financial advisors that is just beginning to take hold nationally. There are a few variations of this business model, but all have a good probability of success.

Let us assume that you have an assets under management business model, but realize that I am probably right about clients demanding more value. You decided to convert your assets under management business model to an annual retainer model with a minimum fee of say $2,500.00. The latter way of doing business is instead of charging 1% per year, as an alternative form of compensation is that you charge for the Comprehensive Financial Planning, which includes most if not all of the areas that I described earlier. Depending on the size of the client's net worth, their annual fee would be in the neighborhood of $5,000 or 7,500 per year. If you as the client have more than $1,000,000 in assets, then this is a cost savings to you. Therefore, you are likely to be happy to stay put. This model works for the established advisor with an existing block of customers. They have headed off the cannibalization at the path by tackling it head on.

For smaller net worth households, the annual retainer fee may be in the $2,500 to $5,000 per year range. This way, a financial planner with 100 clients could bring in a minimum of $250,000, which should allow them the time to handle a close relationship with you. It might be great for a financial advisor's ego to have one billion dollars in assets under management, but I guarantee you that this type of advisor does not have time for you.

Therefore, when you are evaluating a financial advisor, you certainly want to see the size of their firm and the number of their clients. If they are too big, then you might get lost in the shuffle. Personally, I think someone who has a limited client base would be more beneficial for clients.

REGISTERED REPRESENTATIVES

Are you a registered representative and FINRA Series licensed? This is the question that you should ask of your financial advisor. If they answer yes, then you know that they are compensated on commissions. This means that if they sell you stocks and bonds, then they will receive a portion of the commission as their compensation. If they sell you a mutual fund, then they will receive a portion of the sales charge as their compensation. If they sell you a variable annuity, then they are compensated by commissions and they receive a portion of the sales charge. If you buy a real estate limited partnership from a registered representative, then you will most likely be paying your registered representative up to 8% in commissions.

Here is a sample commission schedule from a full service brokerage firm and it is already discounted. In other words, they think they are doing you a favor with this schedule.

Transaction Amount	Commission Charge
$0.00 - $3,000	$43 + 1.0% of transaction amount
$3,001 - $10,000	$68 + 0.8% of transaction amount
$10,001 - $50,000	$73 + 0.8% of transaction amount
$50,001 - $100,000	$73 + 0.7% of transaction amount
$100,001 - $200,000	$73 + 0.6% of transaction amount
$200,001 - $300,000	$73 + 0.5% of transaction amount
$300,001 - $500,000	$73 + 0.4% of transaction amount
Over $500,000	$73 + 0.3% of transaction amount

Minimum Charge: $57.00 or .05¢ per share, whichever is greater.
Maximum Charge: $100 for 100 shares or less. See chart above for more than 100 shares.

When you ask your full service broker, what the commission will be for buying stocks, now you can see why they can't answer you right away. They have to go through a bunch of gyrations to figure out your commission. Compare this schedule above to a flat $12.95 up to 5,000 shares. Which one is better for you?

Now you can see why they have a financial incentive to recommend stocks to you. They earn a percentage of the above commissions from their recommendations.

There are independent firms too. Most of these firms also do business on a fee basis in addition to commissions.

The point that I want you to understand is that both types of these firms have a financial incentive to sell you products that produce the most revenue for the firm. The people that work for these firms cannot maintain their role as a financial advisor unless they produce a certain level of revenue. If they do not produce revenue, then they can lose their jobs.

All of these firms may also be dually registered. This means that they are a broker/dealer and a registered investment adviser. The problem with being dually registered is that you as the client have to figure out which hat they are wearing. The question then becomes why should you have to worry whether or not someone is truly doing things in your best interest or not? How they do this is they slide the broker/dealer forms in front of you to sign. It will say Brokerage Account on the form if they are acting as a broker/dealer registered representative. This means that they will be compensated by commissions for this type of account.

In my opinion, I would stay away from FINRA registered representatives. Your interests will be secondary to their affiliated FINRA firm. You can take that to the bank. That is if your bank is still in business.

INSURANCE AGENTS

Insurance companies have their own broker/dealer with registered representatives. Some of those that I am sure that you have heard of are Northwestern Mutual, New York Life, Met Life, Prudential, ING and John Hancock. These are some of the bigger firms, but there are a slew of other insurance company broker/dealers with FINRA registered representatives.

Understand this critical difference between registered representatives who are incented to sell you products and registered investment advisers who do things in your best interests.

Insurance companies have products that we all need that are guaranteed like life insurance, annuities, disability and long term care insurance. There are times when you should do business with an insurance agent. If you do, then make sure that they are also work as a registered investment adviser.

Another thing you could do to protect your interests is use a registered investment adviser and let him or her refer you to an insurance agent that they trust.

I wanted to give you an idea of the compensation paid to insurance agents for life insurance and annuities, since these are their primary products. For term life insurance, commissions can range from 50% of the annual premium up to 100%. The same goes for whole life, universal life and variable life. Except with the latter products, there is a limit called a target premium. If you want to see your insurance agent squirm, then ask them what the target premium is on the product they are recommending. A quick ballpark calculation in your head would be 90% of whatever they tell you is their commission. This is not going to be 100% accurate, but it will be in the ballpark.

If you want to verify that what they are telling you is accurate, then look at the life insurance illustration. At the bottom of most illustrations, you should see the target premium. It may say "TGT 10158.98" or something similar. They try and disguise it, but agents know right where it is, believe me. If you cannot find it, then ask them to point it out.

Annuities fall in a range that depends on whether there is a bonus associated with the product sold. If there is a bonus, then most likely the surrender charge is going to be ten to 15 years or longer. The bonus could be up to 10% paid into the contract to get you to purchase the annuity. The typical commission on a product like this is going to be eight to ten percent.

For a non-bonus annuity, with a shorter surrender charge, you will find the commissions in the four to seven percent range of the premium.

INSURANCE INVESTOR ALERT

If you are being presented a product with a 10% and a 15-year surrender charge, then ask how soon you can annuitize the contract. If they tell you ten years, then I would not buy it. The best annuities, in my opinion allow you to annuitize it after one year. Another thing you want to know is if it has a five-year period certain option. If the minimum period certain option is ten years, then again, I would not buy it.

You always want to be able to gain access to your money as quickly as possible. This is especially true in a recession like we are in here in 2009.

REGISTERED INVESTMENT ADVISERS

Which one is better? FINRA registered representatives, insurance agents or registered investment advisers? Registered investment advisers are the only type of firm that you should ever do business with, albeit with the aforementioned previously described Comprehensive Financial Planning demands.

Think about the current scandals and bailouts with regard to the big banks and Wall Street firms. This old model of generating the most revenue that you can from customers like you is going the way of the do-do bird. I am telling you that doing business with registered investment advisers is where you should be today.

Do not believe the spin being put out by the press with regard to the New York person scandal. They are trying to spin it as if it was all the SEC's fault because his firm was a registered investment adviser. The SEC is a fine organization with outstanding young attorneys. However, the problem is that they need people with compliance backgrounds like me who know what to look for in an audit. The SEC is not a regulator made up of member firms like FINRA. What is a member firm supposed to do? Look after their members. There are lots of problems with the current regulatory environment. I will let Congress sort it all out.

FINRA was the primary regulator for the New York person firm for the last 30 years. As a FINRA regulated firm, they have to submit capital statements every quarter. Long before the New York person firm ever became a registered investment adviser, they were a FINRA supervised firm. So, let me get this straight. The question that I have for FINRA is who was reviewing the quarterly FINRA capital reports? Who was doing the mandatory annual compliance review? Apparently no one. He appears to have gotten a free pass.

Forgive me, but FINRA is the bad regulator in this fiasco. They were in charge of looking at New York person's firm for the last 30 years, doing annual compliance audits and reading those quarterly reports. That means that they saw 120 quarterly reports and never, not even once, noticed any discrepancies. Hockey puck! Those reports were prepared by a hole in the wall accounting firm I hear. That should have thrown up a red flag by itself. It is hard to believe that FINRA can get by unscathed in this scandal. Of course, no one really cares what I think, do they? It just does not seem right to me.

FINRA is a powerful group, however. They just put their former FINRA chairperson in the seat of SEC chairperson. President Obama appointed Mary Shapiro and the Senate confirmed her as the new SEC chairperson. Personally, I do not expect much to change with a ex-FINRA person in charge of the SEC. This is exactly what FINRA wanted. Someone who is partial to their point of view.

I want to see some *perp walks*. I have had enough of the good ole boy network on Wall Street. How about you?

A Different Business Model for Investment Advisers

My suggestion is that your registered investment adviser firm should have no affiliation with any FINRA firm. Thank God for that. The principals should relinquish all associations with FINRA and their FINRA Series 7, 9, 10, 24, 63, 65 licenses. By the way, these are the FINRA licenses that I gave up to be an investment adviser. This firm should be registered as a registered investment adviser in a state, or with the SEC. They should do what I love to do and that is Comprehensive Financial Planning.

They may charge an initial fee for the Financial Plan. In order to keep their clients on track, they will provide their clients with Portfolio Management reporting. Portfolio Management reporting is really why you are paying an assets under management investment advisor. It certainly could not be their great performance for the last few years.

Okay, I know what you are asking. What is the catch? There is no catch. They charge somewhere between $2,000 and $2,500 initially, for preparing the Comprehensive Financial Plan. Then, they charge a quarterly retainer of $1,000 to $2,000. They discount the fee to groups and companies. (They reserve the right to raise their fees based on supply and demand. Isn't supply and demand part of the business cycle?) The only catch is do they know what they are doing?

This business model will allow them to put on around one hundred to one hundred fifty families, hire one or two folks, and enjoy the rest of their life with their clients as their "go-to-guy or girl". If each of the advisors in their firm does the same, then they will have a nice business that can make them proud.

Think about all that help you got with your 401(k). Think about the B shares that you still hold and do not know what to do about them. Think about that $5,000 or more that you are currently paying an investment advisor every year, which has turned out to not be for performance, but for performance reporting. Now there is a better solution.

Comprehensive Financial Planning is what you should receive from your advisor. This is what I do for you.

Background Checks

Today there are a myriad of different titles and professional designations that are used when doing business with a financial professional. I am not going to even try to explain all the different titles and professional designation to you. There are simply way too many to describe. I would have to write another two hundred pages in order to explain them all. Therefore, in the interest of simplicity, I will teach you what you need to know when dealing with a financial professional.

First, you have to understand the three main areas of regulation regarding financial professionals. I want to go into a little more depth concerning registered representatives, insurance agents and registered investment advisers. Forgive me if I seem a little repetitive here, but I think you will see my point at the end of this chapter.

There are three main types of financial professionals. Insurance agents are regulated by the state in which they do business. Another type is a securities licensed professional who maintains one or more FINRA Series licenses which makes him/her a registered representative. Lastly, there are the registered investment advisers who are regulated by the states that they do business in or by the (SEC) Securities and Exchange Commission depending on their assets under management. If someone represents a registered investment adviser, then they do so as an investment adviser representative.

The funny part of all this is that insurance agents never refer to themselves as insurance agents. Further, FINRA registered representatives never refer to themselves as registered representatives. Lastly, investment adviser representatives rarely refer to themselves as investment adviser representatives. Instead, they all call themselves something similar like financial advisors. This is the major problem for potential clients. They all claim to be financial advisors.

It can get even more confusing. Insurance agents can also be FINRA registered representatives and affiliated with a registered investment adviser. They can be regulated by a state insurance department, a state securities department or the SEC. Conversely, they can be an insurance agent only. Alternatively, they can be an insurance agent and a registered investment adviser and not licensed with FINRA.

FINRA registered representatives can also be insurance agents and registered investment advisers. On the other hand, they can just be FINRA licensed and insurance licensed but not registered as a registered investment adviser.

Investment adviser representatives of a registered investment adviser can also be a FINRA registered representative and an insurance agent. Alternatively, they can be a registered investment adviser and an insurance agent. Most of them are registered investment advisers only.

Agency Relationships, Suitability and Fiduciary Liability

You see how this can be very confusing. I was confused writing about it. As a potential client, what you need to know is the difference between agency relationships, suitability and fiduciary. An insurance agent has the legal liability to represent the insurance company first. They are an agent of the insurance company. Therefore, you as a client of an insurance agent will find that your best interests are secondary to both the insurance company and the insurance agent. They have an agency relationship.

A FINRA registered representative has to sell products to keep their position as a registered representative. The business model of all FINRA affiliated firms is to generate commissions and occasionally fees to benefit the FINRA affiliated firm itself. These registered representatives need only recommend suitable investments to you. You need to get this point:

They do not have to recommend anything that is in your best interests.

Their recommendations only have to be suitable. You must understand this critical point. There is no possible recommendation that you will ever receive from a FINRA registered representative that has to be in your best interests.

Keep in mind FINRA is who regulated New York person's broker/dealer. They did not look out for people and charities with millions of dollars. Do you think they are going to look out for you if you only have a few hundred thousand?

Do not misunderstand me. There are some good people who are

affiliated with FINRA affiliated firms who try to do the right thing by you. However, they must produce sales and enough of those sales to keep their offices, their secretaries, their computers, their marketing stipends and on and on. The bottom line is if they treat you right and they are a FINRA registered representative, then they are doing so because of their own personal ethics.

I will give you an example. Let us assume that you do business with a FINRA registered representative and they are five thousand dollars in commissions away from meeting their quota for the year. They may lose their office stipend if they fail to reach this goal. They are going to look for a client in their book of business that they can generate five thousand dollars in commissions before the end of the year.

What they will probably do is look for someone in their client book who is nearing the end of their surrender charge period on their variable annuity. Perhaps, they find a new annuity with a 5% or 10% bonus, which in their mind would help offset any surrender penalty that their client might still have to pay. As the client, you trust your advisor. They recommend the switch of annuities to you. As a result, you receive a new annuity albeit with a little extra bonus, but with a completely new surrender charge period. The FINRA registered representative makes their year-end quota at your expense. This happens all the time.

Insurance agents do the same thing, except perhaps with equity-indexed annuities. In their situation, they may only be $5,000 in commissions away from a free trip to Cancun. They switch one annuity for an equity-indexed annuity to meet their quota. Again, whom does it benefit? The insurance company and the insurance agent are the ones who benefit, not you.

Registered investment advisers are actually the firm, not the person. What I mean is if John Smith works at ABC Investment, then John Smith is an investment adviser representative and his firm is the registered investment adviser. No person can ever be a registered investment adviser, only a firm can be one.

Investment adviser representatives have a fiduciary duty to recommend what is in your best interests. Even if they are insurance licensed, they must make recommendations that are in your best interests. Even if they happen to also be FINRA registered representatives and they are acting as a registered investment adviser, then they must act in your best interests.

However, here is the rub if you will. FINRA firms have a loophole. What they do is get you to sign account paperwork that says that they are acting as a FINRA firm and not a registered investment adviser. Therefore, if you are dealing with a FINRA registered investment adviser, you must scrutinize the paperwork fine print to find this clause. If you are opening a *brokerage* account, then you are most likely not getting the fiduciary protections afforded to clients of registered investment advisers. You must be signing an investment advisory agreement or contract and receive a copy of their Form ADV II or disclosure brochure.

Registered investment advisers disclose or are required to disclose their conflicts of interest in their Form ADV II or disclosure brochure. They will spell it out for you in black and white. If they earn commissions for insurance, then they must tell you and how much. If they offer brokerage accounts instead of investment advisory accounts, then they must tell you in writing. If they win trips and travel awards for selling a certain amount of insurance, then they must tell you in writing. They also must disclose their background and disciplinary history.

Insurance agents do not have to disclose their disciplinary background. FINRA registered representatives do not have to disclose their disciplinary background. Registered investment advisers *do* have to disclose their disciplinary background.

Do you see this critical difference? This is a huge difference. But wait, just when you think that you have it all figured out, there is a catch. If you are a principal of a registered investment adviser, then you have to disclose your disciplinary history to all clients and future clients. However, if you are not a principal of a registered investment adviser firm and you are just one of the many investment adviser representatives, then you *do not* have to disclose your background in writing. A principal is an officer of the firm.

The SEC is formulating new disclosure requirements whereby *anyone* who works for a registered investment adviser would be required to disclose their disciplinary history. I have to question why this was ever allowed in the first place.

Here is another problem. If I am an ex-FINRA registered representative and two years or more has passed since I resigned or was terminated from the FINRA broker/dealer, then any disciplinary history that I had with FINRA will not show up if I am now affiliated with a registered investment adviser. Can you believe that? I guess I have to spell it out in order to get the proper changes enacted.

We need one disciplinary disclosure system for all insurance agents, FINRA registered representatives and investment adviser representatives of registered investment advisers.

It is that simple. Everyone who has an insurance license, or once held an insurance license should have his or her disciplinary history disclosed. Everyone who is a FINRA registered representative or who in the past was a FINRA registered representative should have his or her disciplinary history disclosed. Everyone who is an investment adviser representative for a registered investment adviser should have his or her disciplinary history disclosed.

They way it stands now, an insurance agent who had his FINRA licenses revoked can hire someone to run a registered investment adviser business (hold the requisite licenses) and continue to represent themselves to the public as a financial advisor. Even though they lost their FINRA licenses? Yes, that is, as long as they can get away with it. Unscrupulous advisors eventually get caught. The problem is, however, if you failed to do a background check on them, then that is your own fault. You have to do the background checks people. Otherwise, you are liable to get your heads taken off by these unscrupulous advisors. Once it hits the news, you are just one of many people like the victims of the New York person scandal. What position are you in at that point? Believe me, not a good one.

There are other examples of abuse. Sometimes, the regulators do catch the bad people but they keep doing business anyway. They simple move to a new city or a new office location and keep representing themselves as financial advisors. Or, the classic one for stupidity is that they put everything in their wife's name. How stupid is that? Do they think the regulators are not aware of this folly?

The bottom line is nowadays, you have to check your insurance agent, and FINRA registered representative or investment adviser representative's disciplinary background. It can be a callous thing not to do so! Check them out!

Where to obtain background information on a CFP®, an insurance agent, financial advisor or real estate agent.

Certified Financial Planners

To find info on Certified Financial Planners, visit this Web site: www. cfp.net/search

Registered Representatives (FINRA Series Licenses)

To find info on FINRA registered representatives, visit this Web site: http://brokercheck.finra.org/Search/Search.aspx . (You cannot find info on investment adviser representatives here.)

Registered Investment Adviser Firms

To find info on registered investment adviser firms, visit this Web site: http://www.adviserinfo.sec.gov/IAPD/Content/Search/iapd_OrgSearch.aspx (You cannot find info on investment adviser representatives who are not principals or the owner of their firm here.)

Insurance Agents and Real Estate Agents

Each state has their own Web site for insurance agents and real estate agents. You must contact the state that you do business in for this information. Since, I live and work in Florida, I am licensed in Florida. Here is where you can find info on me regarding my insurance and real estate licenses. The State of Florida updates their Web sites from time to time; therefore, these web addresses were accurate as of the writing of this book. They may change in the future depending on future web updates.

Florida Insurance Agents

To find info on Florida Insurance Agents, visit this Web site: http://www.myfloridacfo.com/data/aar_alis1/

Florida Real Estate Agents

To find info on Florida Real Estate Agents, visit this Web site: www.myflorida.com/dbpr

Non-Regulator Organizations

The National Ethics Bureau has a Web site located at www.ethicscheck.com. This is where you can find info on advisors who pay to be members. They can be insurance agents, FINRA registered representatives, investment adviser representatives, real estate agents, mortgage brokers or accountants or any combination of the above. These individuals are subject to a seven-year background check.

This is not an all-inclusive list. You must go the extra mile and do your homework. I wanted to provide you with what you need to get started. Some states, like Florida have a disciplinary background database that you can search by last name. The hyperlink address above only shows if they are actively licensed. In order to find out if they have a disciplinary background, you would have to search their online database of disciplinary infractions. Conversely, you can always call your state insurance department to verify the background of someone whom you are doing business. Be careful out there.

Recent Scandals & Investment Performance

Think plain vanilla. There is nothing wrong with plain vanilla. In the grand scheme of things, investing done successfully is very boring. It is not exciting at all. People get bored with the mundane aspects of true investing. When people get bored, they look for something exciting to do. Unscrupulous advisors prey on people looking for something different.

Here is the rub if you will. As an investor, you want to make a great return. Most often, the first thing out of your mouth is a question about an adviser's investment performance. If I were to tell you that I average 5 or 6 percent a year, is that going to get you excited about doing business with me? If on the other hand, I were to tell you that I can get you 10 to 12% a year, because I have a special way of investing that involves hedging strategies that are proprietary to our firm, would that peak your interest?

The problem is that all an unscrupulous adviser has to do is blow smoke up your skirt in order to get your attention. The more outlandish or grandiose the claim of performance, the more special that adviser appears to you.

Just the other day, a Florida hedge fund manager ran off. It appears that the innocent until proven guilty Mr. Florida person may have something to answer for concerning his investors' money. Only time will tell.

A few weeks prior to that, I saw a picture of a financial advisor with his ex-wife in front of a fancy car and an executive jet. It kind of makes you wonder why any investor would think about investing with a flashy advisor like that. They are selfish and their personal values are out of whack.

It will take a long time before they sort out all the issues surrounding these cases. Meanwhile, investors are the ones who lose.

Listen to me. With my business model, it is rare that anyone ever writes me a check. Most all of our transactions are done through Charles Schwab and the account transfer system between other firms. In other words, if you come to me with an account at Edward Jones for example, we would just fill out paperwork to transfer your account from Edward Jones to Charles Schwab. I would never touch it, nor would I have access to it, except to do three things. One is that you would grant me the ability to trade the account or make the buys and sells. The second thing that I would be able to do is send your money to your bank account upon your request. It cannot go anywhere but to your bank account and this service is optional. If you do not want it, then it cannot be done. The third thing that I can do is deduct my management fee each quarter as agreed to in our Investment Advisory Contract.

When you are dealing with an unregistered hedge fund, first, they are not regulated. They can put your money in a pooled fund with everyone else's money. They do not have to tell you where they put your money. They can put some of your money one place and some of it somewhere else, without your approval. These hedge funds typically produce their own statements, which lends itself to abuse. Moreover, the end all to be all is that they do not have to explain anything to you since their hedge fund strategy is a proprietary secret.

You wonder why these people run off with people's money. Because they can, that is why. As an investor, you went away from plain vanilla because that was not good enough. You bought into the hedge fund concept because you felt that you were in an exclusive and very elite circle. The only exclusive and elite circle that you are in is the circle of people who lost their money.

Plain vanilla is a good way to think about investing. Markets go up and markets go down. Nobody beats the market year in and year out. If they tell you that, then they are lying through their teeth.

INVESTMENT PERFORMANCE

There are strict rules with regard to showing performance numbers in the industry. The have to conform to certain standards. Simplistically speaking, an investment advisor would have to take his whole assets under management and annualize the return from point to point. The problems with explaining performance are numerous. First, the only way this makes any kind of sense is if every single client is invested exactly the same way. Of course, this never happens, because clients need to hold certain positions for various reasons. Assume that an advisor has 200 clients total, but this advisor's asset mix is a 60/40 split between stocks and fixed income. Therefore, 40% of an advisor's performance numbers will be skewed towards a more conservative fixed income return.

Conversely, assume an advisor only has 40 clients and they are all heavily invested in the stock market. Also, assume that it happens to have been a very good last five years for the stock market. Consequentially, this advisor's performance would outshine the prior one above. As a client, you would lean toward the advisor with 40 clients, because of the worst reason in the world, performance. Then, after you commit your dollars to this advisor, the stock market tanks and you are left scratching your head wondering what happened.

MORE PERFORMANCE ISSUES

Other advisors have Model Portfolios. They are allowed to show their Model Portfolios as a representative sampling of how they invest their client's money. Lot's of times, they have a pitch book. In this pitch book, they have their Model Portfolios. They are supposed to show you the YTD, 1 year, 3 year, 5 year and since inception performance numbers after their maximum fees have been deducted. What happens is you are only shown the best performing Model Portfolio time period.

This is going to sound strange, but these Model Portfolios are misleading in my opinion, even though they are legal. Here are my thoughts on the subject. If you go to an advisor with a Model Portfolio for the last 5 years with a 10.45% return, then you are liable to be impressed by that statistic. Again, the question becomes what are they invested in. Are they like the advisor above with the 40 clients invested primarily in the stock market? Has the last five years been a good one for stocks? Is this starting to click a little bit?

Here is another way to think about this. Once you see this 10.45% return, then you expect to make 10.45%. The bar of expectations has been set. The gauntlet has been thrown down. If this advisor does not make 10.45% return for you, then you are bolting out the door. Now, I have to ask you. Who is really making the big mistake here?

Let us carry this one-step further. Suppose this Model Portfolio has 15 securities in it. It can be all mutual funds in various assets classes. That particular mix of asset classes happened to have made 10.45% for the last 5 years. Now, it is January 1st. You invest on that day. Another investor invests his or her money on July 1. Both of you have invested in the exact same Model Portfolio in the exact same dollar amount. Both you expect to earn how much? I would guess the same 10.45% return. Now, think back to July of 2008. Let us assume that you invested on July 1st of 2008. It is now December 31, 2008. Instead of making 10.45%, you lost approximately 40% on your account. This is an assumption in order to explain my point.

The other investor decides to invest on January 1, 2009. He buys in at a 40% discount. Going forward, who do you think has the best opportunity to do better? Now, think about that Model Portfolio. Did that Model Portfolio really do anything at all for you? Then, why did you rely on it to make a decision to go with that investment adviser?

I hope you get my point about investment performance numbers and Model Portfolios. They are totally irrelevant when it comes to choosing an investment adviser.

The plan and the process are more important than anything. What is the investment adviser's plan during bull markets? What is their plan during bear markets? Are they like me where they will go to cash when the bear market arrives? On the other hand, do they just sit there like a knot on a log and hope the market will turn around? You need to know if your advisor has ever made the decision to go to cash. If they did, when did they do it and why did they do it.

Prudent diversification still works when combined with making strategic moves to go to cash.

More on Scandals

A word about investment risk is called for in this market. Collateralized debt obligations, auction rate preferred's and the Sub-Prime Crisis are the latest problems plaguing our economy. Here is how it all transpired. Mortgages are sold as packaged investments by investment banking firms. With the recent housing boom, most people bought their new house in the last 5 years. However, the mortgage bankers did not want the good times to end. Loosely regulated as they still are today, they decided that they would come up with negative amortization schedule mortgages and no income verification mortgages. They also were willing to loan up to 150% of your home's value. These are called sub-prime mortgages. Some people call them NINJA loans. NINJA stands for *No Income, No Job* or *Assets*.

After the mortgage bankers sold all this stuff, the investment bankers packaged them up as CDO's or collateralized debt obligations. Investment bankers were stupid enough to buy them and sell them to each other. Then, they borrowed against them with some having leveraged them up to 300 and 400%. Well, as we now know, they all blew up ala Bear Stearns, Lehman Brothers, Citi Group, AIG and Merrill Lynch.

Mostly investment brokerage firms hawked auction rate preferred's (ARS's) as an alternative to money market accounts. These ARS's as they are called are short-term municipal bond issues that got their liquidity from investment bankers. Well when the investment bankers began writing down the billions of dollars in sub-prime loans, the last thing they wanted to do was supply liquidity to short term municipal bond issues. They did not have any liquidity to supply.

Several people will be hurt by this New York person scandal. Large institutions and charities were duped too. Smart people were also duped. People who had no idea that their money was even invested with this person were duped, also. Mr. New York person's firm was a broker/dealer regulated by FINRA. He also had a registered investment adviser filing with the SEC. I personally reviewed this SEC filing and could easily see some red flags in it. New York person's firm was dually registered. Well, unfortunately there were significant failures here and plenty of blame to go around.

FINRA is a self-regulatory organization. This means that people in the broker/dealer industry sit on the committees. Is this a conflict of interest? You tell me.

FINRA had previously audited and fined New York person's firm twice for small amounts, but they failed to uncover the massive fraud involved. I would suggest that FINRA think about hiring forensic accounting experts to audit firms. FINRA is not looking too good right now as far as a regulator. They were supposed to be watching the investment banks and now this New York person scandal has landed on their doorstep.

We are now seeing another wave of Wall Street firm layoffs. Congress, yes the worst one in the history of the United States, the same Congress who does not know how to pass any meaningful legislation except earmarks, has called for congressional hearings. All of these people take money from you guessed it, investment bankers and mortgage bankers. Do you really think anything meaningful is going to happen because of congressional hearings?

I just read a copy of the Emergency Economic Stabilization Act. It is full of earmarks. Go read it if you do not believe me. Just Google it and see for yourself. It has the TARP plan and stuff about wooden arrows in it.

Well, at least we have a new batch of Congressional men and women coming in. I hope that with a little luck, things will improve. Forgive me that was wishful thinking on my part. It looks like Congress is going to pay back all their cronies with a stimulus bill full of pork projects. There is over four billion in there for a community organizer. Four billion? I think we Americans need to raise a little hell with these people in Washington. I do not know if we can ever stop this self-serving bunch of hypocrites from bilking the taxpayers dry, but it is certainly worth a try. Let your local Senators and Congressmen know how you feel.

A Compliance Officer's Viewpoint

While I was working as Chief Compliance Officer at my prior firm, a married couple came in because of a seminar. As part of our service, we routinely review our prospects account statements. I was given this couple's account statements to review. Immediately, it appeared to me that the account statements were fraudulent. We called the client and asked for permission to contact the insurance company whose name was on the statements. I went straight to the Chief Compliance Officer for the insurance company. I explained to him that I believed that a registered representative was preparing fraudulent statements and I was very afraid that this unscrupulous advisor had run off with this client's money.

It did not take too long to find out that my suspicions were correct. I ended up having discussions with some regulatory people and helped the client start the process to recover their funds. Take it from me; sometimes it is good to get a second opinion.

Custodians

Personally, I favor Charles Schwab & Co. Inc. as the custodian of choice for my clients. Other custodians of note are Fidelity Investments (National Financial Services), TD Ameritrade, Scottrade, and Pershing. Bear Stearns was in the custodian business. I am not sure what happened to that arm of their business when they went out. JP Morgan Chase bought them at a fire sale.

Most of these custodians do business with registered investment advisers and some do business with commission based broker/dealers. Schwab has been doing it the longest, they have the most registered investment adviser assets under management and I used to work there for a little over four years, so that is why I like them.

As an investor, you want to know where your money is. When it is with Schwab, there is no question. You can take comfort in knowing that your money is with a reputable firm. When I was the Branch Manager in Jacksonville, I spoke with the Compliance Department almost every day. Schwab is a highly, highly compliance oriented firm. They have some of the best compliance procedures in the industry. Nothing is overlooked. For example, if you send in an application for a new account and the application is not dated, they will not open that account. They will send it back to be properly signed and dated. Schwab has a compliance process and they follow it. They are not a firm that lets things slide. It has to match their process or they will not accept the business. It does not matter how much money an adviser has or how much money a client has. The bottom line is that you have to follow their process and procedures in order to do business with them. There are no loopholes with Schwab. You have to play by their rules.

You can also take comfort in knowing that money cannot leave your account unless it is going to an account in your name. If you want to send it to a third party, then it must have your signature on a form. Then, they check that form's signature for the signature that they have on file for you. If there is a mismatch, then they do not send it. Schwab has no problem making you and me mad over the movement of money. This is a good thing in my mind. Don't you agree?

If you do business with a registered investment adviser that uses Schwab, then you can log on and follow your account. You can see your money 24/7. You can download statements from Schwab and compare them against the statements from your adviser. They should match exactly. Occasionally, there may be a mismatch due to data errors from Schwab and the adviser's software, but most times, it is just a manual data entry error by the adviser's staff. The point is that placing your money with a reputable custodian like Schwab is a smart decision. Placing your money with John Doe Secret Hedge Fund is not a good decision.

REGULATORS OF NOTE

FINRA stands for the Financial Industry National Regulatory Agency. They were formally known as the National Association of Securities Dealers or NASD. All registered representatives are regulated by FINRA. Again, registered representatives are people who are Series 6, 7, 8, 9, 10, 22, or 24 licensed. They may have other FINRA Series licenses like the 63 or 65, too.

FINRA makes money on the number of registered representatives subject to their regulations. Most registered representatives are leaving FINRA firms and choosing to affiliate with registered investment advisers. Others are choosing to sell only insurance and annuities. If they are all bailing out, then FINRA is losing a significant amount of their income. As a result, instead of accepting the reality of the situation, they are exerting their influence and trying to get control of the investment advisers and the insurance agents from a regulatory framework. They have been successful in forcing the SEC to make fixed indexed annuities securities products. Groups of insurance companies are suing the SEC because their own rules say that if it has guarantees, then it is an insurance product. Fixed indexed annuities have guarantees. The court will sort it all out. I guess that is why the SEC put the implementation out to January of 2011.

So far, FINRA has been successful by virtue of getting the SEC to implement this rule. The result is that all insurance agents who were not previously regulated by FINRA would now fall under their regulatory jurisdiction. FINRA stands to gain $50,000,000 a year by having regulatory jurisdiction over fixed indexed annuities. That is per year! Do you think there might be just a wee bit of a conflict of interest here on their part?

FINRA is also trying to get control over investment advisers. FINRA is the organization that was supposed to be watching Bear Stearns, Lehman Brothers, Merrill Lynch, Smith Barney, and UBS, etc. etc. Need I say more? These people have the audacity to want to regulate investment advisers. That is like giving the keys to the prison to the inmates. FINRA, formerly called the NASD, regulated the New York person's firm.

The bottom line is that with FINRA, it is all about the money. There is not a politician or regulator on the planet who knows how to survive on a budget. Look at all of them squealing like stuck pigs for a bailout here in late 2008 and early 2009. They all think that have a right to increase their revenue every year no matter what. In my opinion, FINRA should downsize like everyone else in the world when times get tough. They should stay far away from registered investment advisers.

It is unfathomable to me that the people regulating these brokerage firms, yes the same ones that have single handedly brought down our economy, want us to be subject to their compliance rules! Is that nuts or what? They do not care about watching out for investors. All they care about is keeping their gravy train going. Okay, I will get down from my soapbox.

INVESTMENT POLICY STATEMENTS

There is a lot of ego involved when it comes to investing, especially as it relates to men and their investment decisions. Let us face the facts, men. For the same reason that we do not need a map, we do not need anyone to tell us how to invest. Our egos will guide us right to the proper place.

Even after, we are lost and our wives are telling us to stop and ask for directions, we will have none of that. We know it is around here somewhere and if we drive around long enough, then surely we will find it.

Investing for men, rather works the same way. The blind fool idiots like us who think we can get there without a map, also believe that we can invest without a financial roadmap, or financial plan. Little do we realize that a map for driving directions would help us tremendously, so too would a financial roadmap for our life.

One of the first things that we need to develop is an Investment Policy Statement. This acts as a guide for our overall investment portfolio and keeps us going in the right direction. If it does not match our stated Investment Policy, then we do not invest in it. Some of the things that should be in your Investment Policy Statement are the types of acceptable investments. For example, are stocks allowed, or should we stick with mutual funds? Are Exchanged Traded Funds appropriate? Do we want to follow an Index approach, or an Actively Managed approach? Are Alternative Investments to be considered?

Other things to consider are the amount of risk we are comfortable taking. The anticipated income and expenses that we will have in the future is also a primary concern. The amount of cash and cash equivalents needs to be stated in writing. When will you sell and rebalance your portfolio? All of these issues are best considered up front, before you invest. In addition, they mean more if you put it in writing.

What I want you to focus on is the amount of risk that you have taken in the past and what you may be taking in the future. You will be better off, if you think these things through in advance. The investment policy statement will be your guide.

Here are some sample investment policy statement questions:

Income Requirements

Do you need income from your investments? _____ Yes   _____ No

If so, how much will you need each year? $ _____

How often will you need it?
( ) Monthly ( ) Quarterly   ( ) Other _____

Starting when? _____/_____/_____

Time Horizon

How long do you expect to have this money invested before liquidation or before substantial modifications?

( ) Ten years or more   ( ) Five to ten years   ( ) Three to five years
( ) One year to three years   ( ) Less than one year

Rate of Return Objective

Based on historical results over the last 50 years, it is reasonable to expect the following before tax performance.

Stocks 5 to 9%
Bonds 3 to 5%
CD's- Money Markets - Savings Accounts 0 to 3%

With the above rates of return objectives in mind, what is your before tax rate of return objective for your entire portfolio? _____ %

Tolerance for Stock Market Risk

Investments providing the best returns over time also have been those investments that typically have involved the greatest risk (that is fluctuation of principal or value). The higher the return desired, the greater the risk that usually must be assumed.

On a scale of 1 to 100, how would you rate your tolerance for stock market risk?
(1 is lowest, 100 is highest) _____

Liquidity Requirements

When cash or cash equivalents (money market funds, bank CDs, Treasury bills, and so on, are part of a portfolio, some people want or need a specific portion to remain as cash, so it can easily be drawn upon. What portion of this investment portfolio do you want to maintain as cash?

( ) No minimum liquidity needs (cash is handled separately)
( ) A minimum of _____% of total investments in cash or cash
         equivalents.
( ) At least $_____ in cash or cash equivalents.

What is the maximum percentage of the portfolio that can be invested long-term?
(Five (5) years or longer)

( ) 0%- 10% ( ) 11%-20% ( ) 21%-30% ( ) 31%-40% ( ) 41%-50%
( ) 51%-60% ( ) 61%-70% ( ) 71%-80% ( ) 81%-90% ( ) 91%-100%

Will significant cash withdrawals, savings for retirement, a new home, or college costs, or significant contributions, an inheritance or exercise of stock options, be made in the not to distant future?
    ( ) No   ( ) Yes   If yes, explain _____
_____

Investments and Taxes

Your current federal tax bracket is:
( ) 10%   ( ) 15%   ( ) 25%   ( ) 33%   ( ) 35%

Other tax considerations may include: (Check all that apply)
( ) I may be subject to the Alternative Minimum Tax
( ) I need to reduce current tax levels
( ) I have unused passive losses

( ) I would like to control future taxable income
( ) Taxed managed investments are not as important as taxable investments with potentially attractive returns

Anything Else We Should Know?

Please provide us with any other pertinent information (anticipated Real Estate purchases, legal proceedings, divorce pending, tax considerations, capital gains, promissory notes and so on) that we should know regarding your investment attitudes and requirements that have not been covered by this questionnaire. _____
_____

Amount And Frequency Of Investments/Withdrawals Anticipated

Please estimate the contributions and/or withdrawals, if any, you anticipate making with regard to this account(s):

Year	Contributions	Withdrawals
1	$ _____	$ _____
2	$ _____	$ _____
3	$ _____	$ _____
4	$ _____	$ _____
5	$ _____	$ _____

For Contributions or Withdrawals larger than $10,000 per year, please explain: (For example: Retirement Income Withdrawals, Inheritance expected, Buying or Selling a Business or Buying or Selling Real Estate or Investment Property)

_____

That ought to give you an idea about an Investment Policy Statement. You can get more involved and say you want to invest in only social responsible companies or other restrictive measures. It is all up to you. With an Investment Policy Statement, it makes it clear to both you and your financial advisor what some, but not all of your expectations are, for your business relationship.

DELIVERY OF INVESTMENT ADVICE

I am hungry for financial planning. Let us assume that you are what I described as a passive investor. You really enjoy life and you do not want to spend your evenings getting the red eye looking at your computer.

Just as John Belushi's character Bluto in the movie *Animal House* said, "My suggestion to you is to start drinking heavily". No, I am just kidding. Things are not that bad for passive investors. They can actually be very, very good.

If you are a passive investor, then you will need financial planning. I will talk more about how to pick a professional later on in this book. For now, I want to suggest what type of advisor to go after and the investment choices available through them.

If you have investable assets of less than $100,000, then you can expect to be solicited by a securities licensed life insurance professional, a bank/credit union securities licensed professional, a regional investment firm independent securities professional, or perhaps even one of the major wire house professionals.

If you are a passive investor, you do not want to go directly to a mutual fund family for help with your investments. You need more attention than they will give you. The bottom line is the fact that they just want your money.

In addition, you do not want to go to a discount broker unless you can walk into a branch, sit down, and talk with someone. If you are dealing with someone just over the Internet and the telephone, then this will not work for you.

Some of the aforementioned professionals will help you get started. You will have to pay them via commissions, assuming of course that you do not mind paying commissions.

There are other options available at this level of investable assets.

They are investment advisers with low minimums. Instead of paying a commission, you would pay an annual fee based on the asset size of your account.

These investment advisers would have an account where they can put you in a portfolio of mutual funds, or a portfolio of stocks, ETF's and bonds or a different mix of assets. Occasionally you can find these type of investment advisers with minimums as low as $25,000.

Some of the more sophisticated professionals will have the option of separate account managers. The separate account managers can be mutual fund companies that only manage these accounts for more sophisticated investors who are committed to letting them do their job. There are also the unknown separate account managers who do a superb job. Relatively few people know about them, because they do not market themselves. Either way, your money will be in a quite different pool of funds than your average mutual fund. The average mutual fund will have significantly more money coming and going which makes it more difficult to manage. The separate account managers do not have this headache near as much as their mutual fund brethren do.

The bad news that is now painfully evident after the New York person scandal is that he was in effect a separate account manager. You have probably read or heard about feeder funds. A feeder fund is an investment advisor who holds himself out as the quarterback of your investment portfolio. His job as leader of this feeder fund is to choose the best money managers that he can find for you. Unfortunately, for some people, these feeder fund quarterbacks chose New York person's firm. As a result, the game has changed. I doubt people will be quite as eager to invest in feeder funds as they once were since this scandal.

For the sake of argument, let us assume that you still would like to know more about separately managed accounts. Therefore, I will clue you in a little more.

With your separate account manager choices, you will find bond managers, balanced fund managers, large value managers, large growth managers, small value managers, small growth managers, midcap value managers, midcap growth managers, international managers, non-U.S. managers, sector managers, sector rotational managers, market timers, hedge fund managers and the super top-secret managers.

The difficulty in selecting one of these is the lack of diversification that will surely evolve if you only have $150,000 to invest. Most of these managers have a $100,000 minimum and some have $200,000 or more minimums. Therefore, what you have to think about is do you really want to be that *aggressive* by placing $150,000 in all stocks?

Separate account managers are an alternative, but you probably want to think twice now before investing with them. I doubt that I would commit too much of your portfolio to any one separate account manager. It is just not a smart idea any more. Putting two, three or four million dollars with one manager is not the thing to do any more. The dynamics have changed today. When you think about the alternatives of the recent bear market and you factor in these scandals, then spreading your money around is probably a very smart thing to do.

Let me back up a moment here to those who have under $100,000 again. I have one simple rule for investing that works very well in keeping your portfolio diversified. Never and I mean never let a securities professional suggest that you put 25% into four different funds or areas. Run do not walk out of their office. They are inexperienced and you will have a very unpleasant investment experience if you allow you money to be invested this way.

I see this hypocrisy more prevalent in the variable annuity business. I met with an 80-year-old woman one day who was new to my town and she had been referred to one of the local financial advisors who had a good reputation. This advisor sold her a variable annuity where he personally pocketed $7,000 in commissions. The customer had incurred an 8-year surrender charge on the new variable annuity. Therefore, she could not move it out of there without a penalty of $8,000 in the first year. Then, the financial advisor diversified her $100,000 into $25,000 in a large growth fund, $25,000 into an aggressive growth fund, $25,000 into an international stock fund and the final $25,000 into a bond fund. In two months, she was down over $11,000 and if she wanted to get out it would cost her another $8,000. Therefore, she was looking at almost $20,000 to get away from an inexperienced FINRA registered representative. I advised her to go to the state securities department and complain. How many 80-year-old people do you know that can afford to lose $20,000 in 2 months?

You have to be careful with these people and ask good questions, especially when they have a financial incentive to get your money. When someone wants to take your whole amount of money available to invest and put it all in a variable annuity, then you can bet your bottom dollar that they are thinking only of the commissions that they will be making. Your needs will be noticeably absent from their train of thought.

Professional Advice

This section applies primarily to the passive and the validator type folks. We cannot do everything ourselves, (even if it is cheaper) unless we want to give up our family time. To me that is just not acceptable when you can hire a true professional.

Let us face the reality of the situation for do-it-yourselfers. If you are a do-it-yourselfer, are you really on the job of managing your money 40 hours a week? I did not think so.

Compensation Makes a Difference

First, you have to understand how compensation factors into the mix. The products that you will be offered are contingent on how your financial professional is compensated. There are several ways that financial professionals are compensated. You have to ask these professionals how they are compensated, then this will help you in your decision making process.

One way that financial professionals are compensated is by salary. Yes, that is right. I said salaried. There are some situations where financial professionals are compensated on salary and may have some type of incentive bonus structure on top of that. These types of professionals have a fairly conflict of interest free form of financial planning advice, but the downside is that they have no financial incentive in the performance of your portfolio. Their primary motivation or their incentive package is probably based on getting a certain amount of assets in each quarter with a combination of maintaining a high persistency rate. Persistency means keeping the clients with the firm.

Schwab, Fidelity, TD Ameritrade and Scottrade retail branch offices are examples of financial people on salary. Realistically though, you can generally get some very good counsel from these professionals, especially if you can find a Certified Financial Planner®, or other credentialed financial services professional who is on salary. The way to deal with these salaried professionals is to check in with them at least once a year for a review. Maintain the 20% rule with the stock limitation of 65%. I will write more about the 20%/65% rule in a later section.

The second type of financial professional that I would like to discuss is the one compensated by commissions, or a combination of fees and commissions. Herein lays a conflict of interest. They make money from what you buy from them. This is not all bad, especially if you have less than $100,000 to invest.

For example, let us say you have $50,000 to invest. Your goal is to get to $150,000 in order to get a little better choice of options and investment advice. You find a professional who agrees to commit time and effort in designing a portfolio for you (within the confines of the 20% rule). The price for this is going to be roughly between $2,000 and $2,500 if you go with mutual funds. Independent financial professionals receive 80 to 90% of that commission. Bank, insurance company, and wire house professionals may only receive 30 to 40% of that money.

You have a Hobson's choice choosing between B shares and A shares. A shares have lower expenses and B shares have those darn surrender penalties. Personally, I would choose A shares, because it gives me the most flexibility to make changes as the economy changes. I cannot tell you how many people I have talked to that are in B shares in the first few years and want to get out. They never want to get out bad enough to eat those surrender charges, however. As a result, they stay stuck in the mud with some bad investments.

Forget about C shares if you have less than $100,000. Most financial professionals who are compensated on commissions do not want to do all that work for only their share of $1,000 which may be as little as $300.

Back to my hypothesis that going with a commissioned based financial professional may actually be beneficial if you cannot find a fee compensated investment adviser to help you. Let us assume that you bought A shares. You can still move from value to growth within the fund family without paying any additional commissions. Assuming of course they have both good value funds and good growth funds. In addition, movement among bonds funds is also easy. With regard to bonds, you want choices between ultra-short, short, intermediate and long term. Therefore, your portfolio can change as your needs change.

In addition, if you start out with $50,000, you have paid your commissions in advance. What if your portfolio grows to $100,000 in five to 7 years? Do you have to pay the financial professional any more commission? No, you do not. Unless, you have temporarily bumped into a wall, lost your senses as a result, let your financial professional churn your account, and charge you all new commissions again. If you paid an annual management fee of 1.5 to 2% a year for 7 years while your $50,000 grew into $100,000, then you would undoubtedly pay more than 4 to 5% one time for the A shares.

Therefore, if you do go with a commission based financial service professional, be sure and utilize good mutual fund families with a lot of flexibility in asset classes and styles. You can actually move around within the fund family for a long time and achieve your goals without any additional commissions. The broker may not like it, but you will undoubtedly make some more money somewhere along the way and add to an account or two with them.

The third type of financial service professional is the fee only advisor. Their incentive is to build up "x" number of million dollars in assets under management and have recurring income each year from their clients. They have a financial incentive for your account to grow and stay on the books. The more their block of business grows, the more they are compensated.

The thing to watch out for with these financial professionals is to not be too demanding of their time. They will typically include 2 to 4 free visits a year as a part of their fee. If you call them all the time questioning what they are doing, then they will jettison you and your accounts out the door. I am very serious about this. They will do this. Give them respect and give them time.

I probably would pay close attention to the financial advisor's Form ADV II. This is their disclosure document that tells you how they invest, their fees and their financial background.

In addition, I would probably prefer to see a more seasoned financial advisory shop with at least $10,000,000 in assets under management. If they have this amount in assets under management, they have it because something is working. They are generally less inclined to have financial pressures to bring in new assets and may be inclined to limit their addition of new clients.

These types of financial service professionals have a style of management. You need to find out what that style is. It could be growth, value, sector rotation, bonds, or a multitude of other options. They could invest in regular mutual funds, institutional mutual funds, index funds, Exchange Traded Funds, individual stocks, bonds, or any combination of the above.

These professionals are going to tell you that they have a better idea and its okay for you to be *aggressive;* especially when you tell them, you have a 10-year time horizon. There are ways to combat this, however. Stay with a balanced approach, if you have less than $200,000. As an alternative, let the professional manage the stock portion of your account and you manage the bond portion. This way you can keep the 65% stock rule in play.

If you have between $200,000 and $300,000, then you can do the 65% stock rule a little easier. The only thing you need to make sure of is that they are not a feeder fund sending your money to someone like the innocent until proven guilty New York person.

Again, these professionals are going to want all of your money. That is their incentive. Start out with what turns out to be 65% (or less depending on how much risk you will be taking) of your portfolio. In reality, if they do a good job, your 65% may grow to 70% of your overall portfolio in a year or two. When that happens, you need to move it back down to 65%. A seasoned financial professional should understand what you are trying to accomplish. It is simple. It is called re-balancing your portfolio.

A more recent entry into the field of financial advisor compensation is a flat fee arrangement. Some forward thinking financial advisors realize that sometimes it is difficult in a bear market to justify an ongoing assets under management fee. Let us face it; people do not want to pay 1% when they lost 40%. Nor, do investors with $5,000,000 want to pay a financial advisor .50% a year, which is $25,000 or more a year, especially after all these scandals. Somehow, it just does not seem worth it to them.

Therefore, these new financial advisors charge a flat fee for their services. Typically, this will include financial plans, tax planning, and estate planning in addition to investment planning. Personally, I believe this has the makings of a great business model. They have a minimum fee and they know they can count on the recurring revenue that they need to function successfully. The client is not getting a rising bill every year. It works for both parties.

There is also another form of compensation, or lack of it may be a better way to describe it. This is called do-it-yourself investing. Do not get your hopes up. There will be a price to be paid.

THE 20%/65% RULE

It is all in the style selection. Who is to argue with Modern Portfolio Theory? Well, there are those who do, but they have good intentions bless their heart. They typically want to improve it somehow. Generally, the opponents of MPT talk about things like a portfolio optimizer in the wrong hands can do a lot of harm. I would agree wholeheartedly with that statement. However, diversification is at the heart of Modern Portfolio Theory and being diversified is not a bad way to go, in my opinion.

What is a portfolio optimizer you ask? It is a sophisticated software program where you put in your current investments and it analyzes your portfolio for the efficient frontier.

What is an efficient frontier? It is a statistical graph that shows that your mix of assets only has certain possible combinations to produce returns. By raising the percentages of your lowest risk investments and lowering the percentage of your higher risk investments, you can determine where you are on the risk axis or return axis.

What is the risk axis, or the return axis? The risk axis is the horizontal portion of the statistical graph that shows how much risk a given portfolio is taking at different levels of the efficient frontier. The return axis is the vertical portion of the statistical graph that shows how much return a given portfolio should have at different levels of the efficient frontier.

Wait just a minute. Why am I explaining all this stuff? Now you can understand why some in my profession say that a portfolio optimizer in the wrong hands is an accident waiting to happen. This stuff gets very complicated very quick. You do have to know what you are doing. If an inexperienced person was to make incorrect assumptions about the asset class benchmarks, then the whole thing falls apart like a house of cards.

Modern Portfolio Theory is Nobel Prize winning stuff, however. Modern Portfolio Theory, or MPT, if done correctly will work very well in up markets and in down markets. This is not to say that you will never have a down year, because even with MPT you will.

In 2008, we proved that there are times when everything goes down. If you feel like Elmer Fudd and say, "there's something screwy going on around here", then it might be time to sell. The trick with regard to MPT is to not be too aggressive and do not be afraid to go to cash sometimes when things are "screwy".

There are two different factions of MPT followers. One group says to diversify across and within asset classes/styles and rebalance periodically (annually, semi-annually, or quarterly.) The other faction says to diversify across and within asset classes/styles and move relative to the conditions of the market and the business cycle. I am somewhat partial to this group myself, even though I know some academics may disagree with my position. However, I am not afraid to take a stand. I proved my point with this approach on October 6, 2008 when I moved our clients to cash. That decision has proven to have kept an additional twenty percent plus in losses from happening to our clients. Did your advisor do that?

MPT states that asset classes or styles tend to perform differently than each other to a degree. A large company value stock or fund will move very similarly with a growth and income fund. However, a large company value fund will move very different from a short-term bond fund.

The technical jargon is called correlation coefficients. This just means that if you design your portfolio with a bunch of investments that are correlated with the S&P 500™, and then your portfolio is going to do what the S&P 500™ does more than likely. If on the other hand, you have a portfolio that has assets that are not all correlated together, then you will achieve more diversification.

The goal of MPT is to design a portfolio that tries to achieve market returns with less risk. Less risk means being less *aggressive*. This is good by the way.

MPT is not static. It is constantly changing. However, at any point in time, there are differences in how a portfolio should be designed. For example, in a depression, or a recession, high yield bonds tend to have higher default rates. Should it be in your portfolio as we are heading into a prolonged recession? I doubt it.

When interest rates are declining, wouldn't you think that Real Estate Investment Trusts would benefit? They sign leases with their tenants for a lot higher rates generally than the current interest rate environment. Then, they pay dividends from those leases. Look at the dividend yields here in late 2008 for REIT's. They are looking attractive. Typically, REIT's pay good dividend rates, but they are significantly more appealing when rates are declining. This would cause their stock prices to increase. Therefore, they should be in your portfolio in situations like those that I just described. Do not get all worked up. Its just one man's opinion, that is all.

The point is...at any particular time in history, your MPT designed portfolio is going to look different depending on how our economy is performing and where we are in the business cycle. Remember that business cycle thing, because it has a bearing on your investments. If you invested with me last year and your friend this year, then their portfolio is going to look a whole lot different from yours. So, keep that in mind.

You should start with the macro view. Look at the following asset classes first to determine whether in the current business cycle and state of the economy they should be included in your portfolio. I have listed them here with their percentage of your portfolio limits.

Asset Style/Class	% Limit
Large Company Value	20%
Large Company Growth	20%
Midcap Value	20%
Midcap Growth	20%
Small Cap Value	20%
Small Cap Growth	20%
Micro Cap Stocks	5%
International Large (includes U.S.)	20%
International Small (includes U.S.)	5%
Foreign (Non – U.S.)	20%
Preferred Stocks/Equity Income	10%
Money Markets	100%
Mortgages	10%
Ultra Short Corporate Bonds	10%
Short Term Corporate Bonds	10%
Intermediate Term Corporate Bonds	10%
Long Term Corporate Bonds	10%
High Yield Corporate Bonds	10%
Ultra Short Government Bonds	20%
Short Term Government Bonds	20%
Intermediate Term Governments	20%
Long Term Government Bonds	20%
Inflation Bonds	20%
Municipal Bonds	20%
CD's	100%

Real Estate Investment Trusts	10%
Natural Resources/Tangible Assets	10%
International Bonds	5%
International Inflation Bonds	5%
Emerging Markets Bonds	5%
Emerging Markets Stocks	5%
Hedge/Market Neutral	20%
Annuities	100%

Inverse Index Funds can be used to offset or neutralize a portfolio. However, when you use these, then you in effect market timing. If you are market timing, then you have to jump in and jump out of these. In order to neutralize your holdings, what you can do is buy an inverse index fund in the same percentage that you have in a regular index. For example, if you have 15% in an S&P 500 index ETF, then you can neutralize it by buying an inverse S&P 500 index ETF. This will effectively neutralize that position, so it neither goes up or down very much at all. Again, you would not want to do this all the time, but it might be appropriate to stem some losses in a quickly falling market.

Two things immediately jump out at you in regard to the above list of asset classes. This does not add up to 100% and there is not more than 20% in any asset class/style with the exception of Money Market funds, CD's and Annuities. It is hard to get hurt by moving to Money Market funds, CD's and Annuities. You will be sacrificing higher returns in bull markets however. Alternatively, when it is a year like 2008, then being in those asset classes might be a good idea.

My first rule is never ever put more than 20% in any asset class/style. The second rule is never put more than 65% in stocks. Both of these rules apply at the same time. In other words, never ever put 65% or more in stock funds, or stocks. If you want to be 65% in stocks, then choose between the above asset classes and be diversified in the process.

In a good economy, buy growth. In a recessionary economy, buy value. Move between value and growth as the economy strengthens or weakens.

Nevertheless, 65% stocks and the rest bonds, annuities and cash may seem to be moderate doesn't it? No, it most certainly does not. Back in the day, this was an *aggressive* portfolio. Today, an *aggressive* portfolio is 80 to 100% stocks. It bothers me that the powers to be still believe that an 80 to 100% stock portfolio is *aggressive*. I do not care what they say. If you are 80 to 100% in stocks for any extended period, then you are going to experience a significant decline in the value of your portfolio. You can put it on the board. Need I remind you about the year 2008?

The goal in designing a portfolio should not be to try to achieve the highest performance possible. It is to try to achieve market returns with less risk. In order to be successful doing this, you have to be very smart about how you put this portfolio together.

If I did want to be 65% stocks, in a recessionary environment, (which would mean that I am losing my mind) then I would probably go with a mix similar to this:

Large Company Value	10%
Midcap Value	10%
Small Cap Value	10%
International Large Company	10%
Emerging Markets	5%
Real Estate Investment Trusts	10%
Natural Resources/Hard Assets	10%
Total	65%

Of course, this is hypothetical and not typical of what I would do every time and for each person. In recessionary times, I doubt very seriously if I would want more than 50% in stocks. I am assuming that you beat me over the head telling me that you want to be *aggressive*. I would try very hard to talk you out of it however. You can count on that.

Disclaimer: Regardless of whether or not it was a growth economy or a recessionary economy, I would custom design every portfolio for each person, or family after significant discussions centered on their individual values, needs and goals. In addition, I would take into account future contributions, expenditures, and withdrawal needs.

In a growth economy, I may design the stock portion of the portfolio in another manner with the above-mentioned disclaimer:

Large Company Growth	10%
Midcap Growth	10%
Small Company Growth	10%
International Large Company	10%
Emerging Markets	5%
Real Estate	10%
Preferred Stocks/Equity Income	10%
Total	65%

I would reduce these percentages accordingly, depending on whether I determined that you needed 50% stocks, 40% stocks, or even 20% stocks. Again, it would depend on where we were in the current business cycle and the current economic conditions. I would move back and forth between the two styles as the economic conditions change. For example, when the Federal Reserve just raised interest rates for the second or third time in a row, it is probably a good idea to take some growth stocks off the table. After all, they are putting the breaks on the economy.

Remember if the economy is slowing down, then this means value. Of course, if the opposite is true and the economy is growing, then this means growth. It is not that hard to figure out. You have to think dynamically and be nimble.

Today, the best way to go is with Exchange Traded Funds, because they have an index fund for each of the asset classes that I listed above. I would build the portfolio with 10 to 14 ETF's, all of which are index funds based on specific asset classes. They are diversified. They have low expenses and it is much easier to control the tax efficiency for non-qualified accounts. In addition, if you need to go to cash, then you can do so when the market is open. With mutual funds, you are stuck until the market closes. Who knows how much more you would lose by having to wait until the market closes?

THE BOND FACTOR

A general rule is that if you have $50,000 or more to invest in bonds, and then invest in individual bonds. If you have less than $50,000, then invest in bond mutual funds. You can save expenses by buying individual bonds when you have more than $50,000 to invest. This is the principle behind this reasoning: Mutual funds have ongoing annual expenses. Individual bonds do not.

Now however, with the advent of Exchange Traded Funds, there are very low expense choices in the bond categories that you need. These choices are tax efficient. In addition, they trade like a stock from a tax perspective.

It all depends on your dollars to invest, your cash flow and expected investment contributions into bonds that will determine whether to go with individual bonds, mutual funds, or Exchange Trade Funds. When I discuss how to put your bonds portfolio together below, then keep in mind that I could be talking about individual bonds, mutual funds or Exchange Traded Funds.

First, you want to look at the big picture. Are you in a high tax bracket? If so, then you may want to incorporate some Municipal Bonds in your portfolio. Secondarily, you want to look at the economy. If rates are declining, then it is a good time to buy bonds. If rates are rising, then it is not a good time to buy them. You do not want to buy bonds at the lowest point in the interest rate cycle. You want to buy them at a higher point in the interest rate cycle. This is of course if you can keep them for a long time horizon.

A SHORT-TERM VIEW

What do you do when CD's are 2.00%, Money Markets are 0.75%, 2 year Treasuries are 1.00%, and 2 to 5 year corporate bonds are less than

4.00%? History does repeat itself. These were the rates in the early 2000's. Look here again in 2008 and 2009. The rates are back down to the same levels.

The first thing you should do is match your bond portfolio as best as you can to your time horizon of when you will need the money. In other words, design it so you get your principal back, when you will need the money. Because, in reality, who knows what is going to happen down the road. The best we can do is to make a good plan.

If your time horizon is less than three years, then you probably want to stay with CD's, Money Markets, Short-term Treasuries and Short-term Corporate bonds, or Short-term Municipals. Match your dollars to your time horizon and settle for the current rate of interest on these investments.

Do not reach for yield and put your money at more risk. Just accept the fact that you are no longer an *aggressive* investor and take your medicine. Your medicine is low interest rates and capital preservation. You are being *aggressive* enough with the stock portion of your portfolio, whatever that percentage may be.

An Intermediate-term View

If you can go out longer with your bond portfolio, then stagger it. Buy a bond that matures each year starting in one year until your time horizon ends. In other words, for a six-year term time horizon where you need a lump sum in 6 years, you would buy a 1-year bond, a 2-year bond, a 3-year bond, a 4-year bond, a 5-year bond, and a 6-year bond. You may be able to design this so you get a check a month.

When the 1-year bond matures, buy another 5 year. When the 2-year bond matures, buy another 4 year. When the 3-year bond matures, buy another 3 year. When the 4-year bond matures, buy another 2 year. When the 5-year bond matures, buy another 1 year.

At the end of this time, you will have your lump sum. Your overall interest rate will depend on what happens to the economy during those six years. Can you control the economy yourself? No, of course not, but, you can control the capital preservation of your bond portfolio and build in a nice return in the process. Another advantage here is that you are unconcerned with the fluctuations of your bond portfolio. It does not matter what interest rates do since you have a stated goal and a stated need in six years.

A Regular Ladder Strategy

If you just wanted a regular ladder strategy, then over the same six-year period you would do the following. When the 1-year bond matures, buy another 1-year bond. When the 2-year bond matures, you would buy another 2 year and so on. This would mean that you have money to reinvest each year. At some point, you would want to end this ladder and that would be at retirement when you need an income stream.

What if you put it all in 6-year bonds, or a bond mutual fund? You would be putting your bond portfolio at risk of losing money if anywhere during that six-year period you needed money. Let us suppose that something came up and you needed money in year three. Your 6-year bonds are paying 6% and now three years later the current rate on bonds is 8%. Who is going to want to buy your 6% bond? Nobody unless you discount it to make it equivalent to an 8% return. Moreover, that will cost you money. With the ladder strategy mentioned before, you will always have something maturing every year, which gives you more options.

The thing to think about with bonds is to pick good quality. In a recessionary environment, you will find companies that are doing poorly will generally have the highest interest paying bonds. It does not take a smart fellow to figure out that these people need the money to operate. Therefore, they are trying to entice investors to buy their bonds. There is risk in individual bond selection, so you have to use your noggin. If a company is doing very poorly and for the near future, it looks like they will continue to do poorly, then you may want to ask yourself, "Do I really want to buy this bond?" Now that I am thinking of it, General Motors comes to mind.

Take the time to think about the business cycle, the company issuing the bonds, and the quality of the company's bonds.

In a bond mutual fund, if interest rates went up after you invested in one, then it really would not be much different. Again, your bond mutual fund would be holding primarily lower yielding bonds in a market where the current yields are higher than the bond mutual portfolio. Therefore, the bond fund manager would have the same problem as mentioned above. He or she may have to liquidate some bonds at the most inopportune time. The result would be that your bond fund net asset value would be lower, when you need the money.

Other Alternatives

Another alternative in the fixed income area is hybrid preferred's.

These are preferred stocks that act like fixed income type investments and are issued by corporations. They usually have a very long maturity of say 25, 30, or even 50 years. Typically, they have a 5-year call feature. In addition, they have an extraordinary call feature, which means that the issuer can call them at any time for par value. They are priced at $25 a share normally upon their IPO. Their price fluctuates like bonds.

For example, when your hybrid preferred is paying 7.5%, and current hybrid preferred rates for the same quality issue is 6.5%, then your price would be at a premium. The opposite is true when you are holding the same 7.5% hybrid preferred and the current rate of interest for the same quality is 8.5%, then your price would be at a discount.

Most of these hybrid preferred's have cumulative dividends. This means that an issuer can suspend dividends for up to five (5) years if they need to. However, they will pay back all missed dividends if they do, assuming of course that they do not go out of business. Therefore, again quality is the name of the game here. In addition, if they do suspend dividends, then you still have to pay taxes on the dividends even though you were not receiving them. Eeek! Well, think of it this way. When you do get all those dividend payments paid up to you, there will be no taxes on the lump sum. Again, assuming they do not go bankrupt. This taxation on ghost dividends is called Original Issue Discount or OID's. You can find out about OID's at the IRS Web site, which is www.irs.gov.

The Bond Portion of your Portfolio

So, don't you see that investing involves many variables outside your and my control? Who knows what interest rates will be 3 or 6 years from now? Nobody. However, do we have visibility about the current trend? Yes, we do. Can we design our portfolio to plan for contingencies? Yes, we can.

Of course, if you only invest 20 or 40% in stocks, then that means the rest of your portfolio will be divided between fixed income and cash. Diversify your fixed income based on the percentage limits that I listed earlier. Use a combination of ultra short, short, intermediate, inflation protected, international bonds and long fixed income choices. Keep enough ultra short and short fixed income to have funds available to move back into stocks when the growth economy returns. If the recession lasts longer, stay short with the portion of stock dollars that you took off the table.

A 40% Bond portion of a portfolio might look something like this:

Cash/Money Markets	5%
Ultra Short Bond	10%
Short Bond	10%
Intermediate Bond	5%
Inflation Protected Bond	5%
Long Term Bond	5%
Total	40%

You can do this with individual bonds, mutual funds or Exchange Traded Funds. The above selection is based on a hypothetical situation with low interest rates. If you had new money to invest and interest rates were high, then you would just put a heavier weighting towards the intermediate and long bond area. If you wanted an international bond exposure, then you would pull 5% from another bond asset class.

Stick to the 20% asset class rule at all costs, even with respect to bond funds. No more than 65% in stocks, too. You will be glad you did.

Of course, you can choose to use fixed annuities for you fixed income portion too. Odds are you are still going to want some in cash though for liquidity purposes.

Less volatility is how you make money. Remember, it is easier to climb out of a shallow hole. You do not make money by being *aggressive* over a longer term time period. Do not let somebody with a Model Portfolio tell you otherwise.

CORE & SATELLITE AND THE PLANET SATURN

There are those who look to the stars for investment help now. Well, sort of. There is a new way of Asset Allocation called, "Core and Satellite". When the brokers/dealers finally figured out that model portfolios did not work, they sent their gurus back to the drawing board. The gurus came up with Core and Satellite as it is known in some circles.

This approach is a more simplistic approach to investing. (We need things to be simple today don't we?) The investment gurus have discovered that most of what they have been doing, *being aggressive,* just simply did not work as they planned. Secretly realizing, the intellectuals that they are I might add that index funds tend to outperform most mutual funds in their corresponding categories. However, this presents an interesting challenge. How can they incorporate index funds and low expense ratio Exchange Traded Funds, into their financial plan? Why it is simple. They looked to the stars and saw the planet Saturn. The gurus realized, the planet could be the index, or core portion of an investment portfolio and the rings around the planet would be the satellite or theme portion. This way, since this is a complex strategy that you cannot put into model portfolio pie charts, then they would be able to justify the fees they charge to create it. Walla! Problem solved.

Broker/dealers and investment advisor are great at reinventing themselves and this is what they have done. They have graduated from model portfolios to what they would have you believe is the more complex Core and Satellite approach. The Core can be the S&P 1500, which is the S&P 500, the S&P Midcap 400, and the S&P Small Cap 600 added together. Okay, this is a quiz. How many of you knew what the S&P 1500 was? That is what I thought!

With this Core and Satellite approach, you have developed international companies, large companies, mid cap companies and small cap companies as your core. Then, for your Satellite portion, you would circle the Core with some individual stocks, sector funds, or other *aggressive* mutual funds in order to round out the portfolio. The thinking is that most of your portfolio will be tied to the market and there will be a floor underneath it for the largest portion of your assets. In other words, you can never do worse than the overall index that you are investing in, because you are buying the index. Further intellectual deductions will help you conclude that most of your performance will be unmanaged. The Satellite portion of your account is where the real value is added according to the gurus.

I wonder. Let us see, if I put 70 to 80% in the S&P 1500, or a group of stocks, or funds that include large companies, midcap companies and small companies, then my performance is going to match the index returns. Okay, wait just a darn minute. Oh, I see it is that valuable counsel that I will be getting on the other 20 to 30% of my portfolio that will make all the difference. Hold the phone, Sherlock. That other 20 to 30% Satellite portion is going to have to really produce some outstanding returns to give me any chance to beat the market. That is a brilliant deduction Watson. You had better be getting a full-blown financial plan with that. Then, the fee might be justified.

The problem that I have with a Core & Satellite approach is that 70 to 80% of it is concentrated in one area. This violates my 20%/65% rule. If it violates my 20%/65% rule, then do not go along with it. The first bear market will expose how bad this strategy performs.

There was a recent study done by one of the major broker/dealers that said investment performance is more important than investment professionals believe. However, finding someone that you can trust was the most important thing by far.

Here is a lesson for every one of you. If you are an investment professional, quit selling performance. The odds are you will not be able to back it up. If on the other hand, you are an investor, quit shopping for performance. You will most likely be extremely disappointed and you are being unrealistic. There are a small handful of professionals who occasionally beat the markets. However, it is very difficult for them to do it consistently.

Remember what I am trying to teach you. In order to beat the markets, you would have to invest a portion of your portfolio *aggressively*. Further, you have to know precisely when the top of the market is and bail out at that moment. In addition, you have to know when to get back in, go to cash, whether to bet on financials, health care, technology, small cap mutual funds, large company mutual funds, midcap mutual funds and on and on. Who can do that consistently? Nobody, not even Warren

Buffett can do it. His Berkshire Hathaway is down a whole bunch, just like most everyone else. On September 18, 2008, BRK.A (Berkshire Hathaway) closed at $147,000 a share. On January 30, 2009, it closed at $89,502.00. That represents a decline of 39.11% according to my trusty HP 12C calculator. The reason Mr. Buffet's Berkshire Hathaway went down this much is because it violated my 20%/65% rule. It is made up of mostly stocks. Mostly stocks violates my 20%/65% rule. Like I said, it doesn't matter if it is Warren Buffet's company.

Do not get depressed. There is a light at the end of the tunnel.

ACTIVE INVESTING

Can I do this? Yes, you can, but again, you need to match your needs to the firm that you choose. For those with under $100,000, commission based firms, or walk in discount brokers are your choice if you are *passive*. Banks, insurance company representatives, independent securities professionals and some wire house representatives are all competing for your business. You can also find some good investment advice for little or no commissions or fees at a few of the largest discount brokers.

No matter where you go with your less than $100,000, always keep one thing in mind. This is your money and you must take some responsibility in order to protect it. You wouldn't hand over your billfold or purse to someone and tell him or her to take whatever he or she want from it, would you? Well, if you do not take some responsibility for your own money, then this is in effect what you are doing.

Keep in mind the 20%/65% rule, follow the business cycle, and keep expenses to a minimum. If you have more than $100,000 to invest, then remember that you can go with a financial advisor and pay an ongoing asset based fee. The financial advisor will usually have someone at the firm to design a portfolio of pre-selected stocks, mutual funds or ETF's from which to choose. The think tank is making all the choices for you.

If you want to do this yourself, do your fund screening based on the economy first. Is the economy growing, or are we headed into a recession? Growth means growth funds, or growth stocks. Recession means value funds, or value stocks. Regardless of where we are in the business cycle, you can do an ETF, mutual fund or stock screen for large company, midcap or small cap stocks. Place your percentages in each of the areas as determined by your *aggressiveness*.

Oh by the way, I can find fifteen studies that say growth is the best place to be and fifteen more studies that say value is the best place to be. The problem with all these studies is they select a specific time period when either growth or value outperforms and slant their study accordingly. These types of studies are meaningless, except for the fact that they show that stocks (whether value or growth) belong in your portfolio. So, do not beat yourself up if you do not time your moves between value and growth just right. The point is to be disciplined with your effort.

When you are looking at ETF's or mutual funds in the stock category, there are several things to consider. One is whether your money is going to be in a taxable or tax deferred account. If you are in a taxable account, then you probably want to look at funds with low turnover ratios as to not incur many capital gains taxes. In a tax-deferred account, turnover does not matter.

Another thing to look at is the total assets under management. Liquidity is the name of the game in mutual funds and ETF's. In the large company area, there are more shares to buy. Should you be concerned if an ETF or mutual fund in this area has four billion dollars in assets? Not necessarily, because there is plenty of liquidity and plenty of large companies to choose from.

Conversely, if you are looking at small companies and an ETF or mutual fund has four billion in assets under management, should you be concerned? Yes, because it makes it difficult to take any position in a small company without the risk of buying more than 10% of the company. Then, the fund manager has to file with the SEC, which lets everyone know what he is doing. Smaller is better with regard to small cap funds.

Midcap funds fall in the middle somewhere. In fact, this category of investing has actually been a good one over the years. It just tends to move in a similar fashion as small cap stocks. You find your differences when you go value or growth.

That reminds me to talk about blend funds. Should you invest in a blend fund? Yes and no. It depends on what type of blend fund it is. If it were an S&P 500 Index fund (which is a large blend) then I would not have any problem with that. You can do better moving from value to growth in the small and midcap area during the business cycle, in my opinion. A blend fund lumps value and growth together. You lose the effectiveness of the differences in performance between value and growth if you do that.

How you can measure it

The beta measurement tells you how the fund or stock measures against the S&P 500. A rating of 1 = the S&P 500. If the S&P 500 returns 10%, a rating of 1.5 means that the fund or stock should return 15%. If the beta is 0.5, then the return should be around 5%, if the S&P 500 returns the same 10%.

If you really want to have some fun, take the 20% rule and add up all your betas. Then, take the weighted average of all your betas and you will see another way to look at how *aggressive* you are being with your picks.

Stock Portfolio	Beta
Average of Large Company Stocks/Funds	1.9
Average of Small Company Stocks/Funds	1.8
Average of Mid Cap Stocks/Funds	1.9
Average of International Stocks/Funds	2.0
Beta Weighted Average for portfolio	1.9

Obviously, if you pick the 65% level for your stocks and your beta-weighted average comes in at 1.9, then, you are being a little too *aggressive*. There is no probably to it. You are being too *aggressive*.

Your beta weighted average target goal for your stocks (funds) should probably really be under 1.4. Remember, the market average is 1.0. After you factor in the bond portion of your portfolio, this will bring your overall portfolio beta down under 1.0 and you will be well on your way to having a portfolio with less risk than the market.

The most important thing about picking ETF's and mutual funds is to stay style specific. Pick ETF's and mutual funds that are true to their style (i.e., large value, large growth, midcap value, short-term bond, etc.) Some mutual funds say they are large growth funds, but when you look at their sector holdings, you will see that they have 50% of their holdings in one sector, like technology. You want to pick style specific funds that actually do what they say they are going to do. That is a novel idea! This is why I like ETF's, because they are *plain vanilla* and they buy the index that they follow. None of that style drift stuff going on in the ETF's like there is in mutual funds.

FOR THE STOCK PICKERS

How do you pick stocks? Well, you do a stock screen. You have to have the software tools to do these screens. The Internet provides a lot of general information, but most of the free stuff is rather inadequate. You probably need to associate with a financial services firm's proprietary software or Internet site like Schwab.

For your stocks screen, you want to look at book values under three, price/earnings ratios of less than 20, price/sales ratios fewer than four, estimated growth rates of more than 20%, return on equity of more than 15%, and a profit margin of more than 10%. Then, if you are looking for large company stocks, select the asset size for large companies in your screen. Do the same for midcap and small cap and complete your screen. This will give you a small group of companies to choose from.

This type of screen is a value screen for stocks that are good values. However, in my opinion, you can also find good growth companies with this same screen. Nevertheless, for those true growth aficionados, all you need to do is raise some of the items in your screen. Growth companies tend to have higher P/E's, higher price to sales ratios, higher growth rates and higher return on equity percentages.

It is very important to keep in mind, if you are picking stocks, then you really should have about $200,000 to invest in the stock portion of your portfolio. If you do not have at least this amount, then I would stick with ETF's until you reach that level. The reason is simple. How many stocks can you buy with $50,000 for example? Not a whole heck of a lot unless you jack up your transaction costs.

It is not a good idea to buy stocks in other than round lots. Round lots are just easier to get better execution on when you sell. You pay more when you have odd lots. This reminds me about dividend reinvestment plans. Dividend reinvestment plans, or Drip's are good for kids. If you are an adult, forget about it. There are better ways to build this mousetrap.

One hundred shares of a $50 stock is five thousand dollars. With my $50,000 portfolio example, you may be able to buy 10 stocks. Is this diversified? No. Is this a risky proposition? I prefer to say it is being too *aggressive.* The risk reward trade off will be high risk and little possibility of reward. You would be off the scale or in the ozone with regard to being *aggressive.* Did I just describe your investment account? Come on, clean that thing up. Quit messing around with your future like this.

With a $200,000 portfolio, you would be able to buy somewhere between 40 and 60 stocks more than likely. Does this have more diversification? Yes, assuming that you do not put it all in tech stocks, which brings me to another point.

There are some major sectors of the economy that you should look at before you design your portfolio. These are Basic Materials, Consumer Cyclicals, Consumer Durables, Industrials, Energy, Utilities, Financials, Health, Technology and Telecommunications. If you are putting together a portfolio of stocks, then do your screens in each of these areas and see what pops up. Again, you have to use common sense. Where are we in the business cycle? Is it a growth economy or a recessionary economy? Are consumers going to buy big-ticket items (Durables) in a recessionary environment? What about retail stocks? Not robustly, I would assume. What about food or drug stocks in a recessionary environment? Now you are thinking! You overweight in the areas that you feel will outperform and underweight in the areas you feel will under perform.

If you are going to buy stocks, then you have to put some thought into it. The better question is when do you sell? There is an inevitable truth when it comes to knowing when to sell a stock.

In order to be successful picking stocks, you have to minimize your losses. The recent bear market has taught us some valuable lessons. One lesson is not to be greedy. A second lesson is not to be stupid. Yet a third lesson is to not ignore reality. A fourth lesson is that there still is a business cycle and there always will be one. Undoubtedly, you can add your own lessons to the mix. Perhaps, the most important lesson of all is to not be afraid to sell.

Everyone is different when it comes to taking losses. Some people can watch 40 to 50% declines in their portfolio and hang on until the bitter end. Others panic at a 5% loss in their portfolio. There is no right answer or set in stone solution as to how much is too much of a loss we can live with. Again, everyone is different, cookie cutter solutions do not help, and all we can do is plan. I would just go back, look at your historical experience on the downside, and ask yourself whether you want to go through that again. If you do not have any historical experience, then set yourself a low downside threshold to test your emotional reaction to a bear market.

If you want to make a good return over the long haul, then you have to minimize those losses. Further, do not be afraid to take a profit either. My suggestion to you is (if you want to pick stocks yourself) to set target sell limits both on the upside and on the downside before you buy. For example, with your XYZ stock that you buy at $50 a share, place a target of $65 on the upside and $45 on the downside. If it hits either price, sell it and do not give it a second thought. Accept your gain or your loss and move on.

If you see that it hit your low target and it is the only stock in your portfolio that went down, and then look for a replacement. If it is one of many stocks that hit your downside sell target, then re-evaluate your whole stock portfolio. You may find that you have several stocks on a downward spiral and you may be able to get out before they all hit your target. If you find yourself in this predicament, then welcome to a bear market, or you may have just discovered that you need professional financial planning advice.

Selling on the upside is the hardest thing. Let us take our $50 stock example. Suppose it hits our target of $65 and we sell. Then, two days later, it pops up to $70. We immediately think we screwed up, because if only we had waited two more days, then we could have pocketed another five dollars a share. This is the great mistake in investing. Quit beating yourself up because you made 30% on your stock when you could have made 40%.

It is okay to take a 30% return off the table. Do not be greedy. You are going to have some successes and some failures in your portfolio. You need to take advantage of all the successes that present themselves to you. Discipline is very, very important. Take your profits, forgot about the stock after that and move on.

Think about it this way. Assume that your stock-picking prowess gives you 50% winners and 50% losers. With your 50% winners, you on average pull off the table 20% gains. Then, with your 50% losers, you on average limit yourself to 10% losses. What is your return? Twenty percent minus ten percent equals ten percent, which is a double-digit return. You only have to be successful half of the time, if you limit your downside risk. Get it?

Again, I personally question why anyone wants to waste the precious days of his or her life doing this kind of thing when professional help is available. Did you lose more than 40% in 2008? If so, then you are fired! You cannot manage your own money any more.

Doing it yourself is not all that it is cracked up to be when compared against the time commitment that you are going to have to make. However, if this is what you want to do and you have the time to do it, then I wish you the best. More power to you my friend.

PASSIVE INVESTING

Help me help you. My apologies go to Tom Cruise's character from the movie *Jerry Maguire*. I am not hanging on by a very thin thread. I do believe that we are accomplishing something here together.

Do you have different goals? Sure you do. You might have a retirement goal, a college education goal, a new house goal, a vacation goal and so on. As a result, you should invest your money in a way that matches your individual goals. There is a catchy phrase for this called Life Goals Planning.

One of the biggest mistakes I see people make, both young and old, is to take emergency fund money and put it in the stock market for a short time hoping that they will hit the jackpot. People, the stock market is not a bank! Do not expect it to act like one, because it never will. Let me repeat that. The stock market is not a bank. Do not ever forget this. Let this be your mantra. If you suddenly have inherited, or accumulated the money for a down payment on a new house, do not invest it in the stock market. Resist at all costs the temptation, even if the market is flying sky high. You have accomplished the goal by accumulating those funds for that new house. Be proud of yourself for accomplishing that goal. That one goal has been achieved. Move onto the next goal. Focus.

Take short-term monies and invest them accordingly. Take medium term monies and invest them for a matching time period. Do the same for long-term dollars. If you need money in six months for a goal, then you have a few choices. These choices are T-Bills, CD's, Money Market funds and perhaps savings accounts. Match the dollars to the need. Take your medicine. Low returns and capital preservation.

Medium or intermediate term goals can be achieved with mostly fixed income choices and perhaps a small percentage in stocks. A three-year goal certainly would not dictate an 80% stock holding. In fact, I would question whether more than 20% in stocks would be appropriate. The risk of loss is too great in such a short-term time horizon. The purpose of any goal should be to achieve it without delay. Taking on extra risk with a three-year time horizon significantly reduces your chances of success. Is it possible? Yes. Is it probable? In rare occasions, if the market happens to go up for the next three years. However, what if it doesn't? What then? Your three-year goal is delayed or missed altogether.

You have to accept reality sometimes. If you have $30,000 and you want $100,000 in three years then you would only need a return of three hundred and some odd percent. No mix of 80% or 100% stocks is going to achieve that. Do not set unrealistic expectations upon yourself. You are just setting yourself up for a big disappointment.

My definition of long-term goals is five years or longer. This is really where you want to put your stock/mutual fund/ETF's/wrap account/separate account dollars. Deciding how much of your investable assets can be put in a long-term goal account is the big question. An analysis must be done of your entire assets. All the short-term dollars must be invested decidedly different from the long-term goals. It is okay to have one account with all of your different time period goals in it. However, you must be focused on how it is allocated towards the individual goals.

If you do go talk with a financial professional, then your meeting should break down the dollars for each of your goals. Take each goal one at a time. Tell the financial professional that you have $30,000 for a down payment on a house and you will need it in six months. Then, let him or her give you the alternatives. If they want to invest it in the stock market, pack your stuff up and walk out the door. They are unprofessional by not listening to what you just said to them.

Once you have taken care of how to invest for the next six months, and then move on to the next goal. Continue this process until you have all of your goals and dollars invested according to your personal needs. Do not forget the 20%/65% rule when it comes to investing. This is your money. Take responsibility for it.

Do not forget about contingencies like life insurance. You do not want it to be a sad day for everybody, do you?

Think of life insurance as a wealth accumulation vehicle, or plan completion insurance. If you cannot make it to the party, then at least your family will. As *Forrest Gump* said, "That's all I have to say about that".

Indexing Alternatives

I wanted to explain a little bit about indexing. There are three main types of indexing today. One is capital weighted. Another is fundamentally weighted and the last is equal weighted.

An example of a cap-weighted index fund in the ETF realm is the iShares S&P 500 Index fund with a ticker symbol of IVV. The S&P 500 is quite simply the 500 largest companies in America ranked by capitalization, or asset size.

An example of fundamental indexing in the ETF universe is Powershares FTSE RAFI US 1000 Portfolio with a ticker symbol of PRF. This ETF is corrected to fundamental factors like sales, cash flow, book value and dividends. These funds tend to pay high dividends and are slanted to more value stocks.

Rydex funds have an ETF with a ticker symbol of RSP, which is based on the equal weighting of the stocks inside. What this means is that the fund buys an equal amount of the stocks inside. In simplistic terms, this means if it has 100 stocks in it and it has $1,000,000 to invest, then it invests $1,000,000 divided by 100 into each stock or $10,000 equally in each stock.

You may be asking yourself which one is the best? Well, there is no easy answer to that question. It depends on what your plan calls for. In other words, if you have chosen a fundamental indexing approach, then your ETF's will be spinning off dividends. If you are trying to minimize taxable income, then perhaps the fundamental indexing approach may not be for you. Instead, you may want to consider a cap-weighted approach, which tends to be more tax efficient. However, cap-weighted funds get all out of whack when the markets are highly volatile. Think back to the tech bubble. As tech companies rose in stock price, this tended to skew cap-weighted indexes toward a larger position in technology. Like I said, there is no easy answer as to which one is the best. It depends on the time frame going in. Which approach might perform more favorably in the future? This is what you want to think about.

You have to stick to your personal needs, goals and objectives. Are you beginning to understand why you need an investment adviser who knows what they are doing?

LIABILITY PLANNING

Reverse Mortgages are also know as HECM's. HECM's are Home Equity Conversion Mortgages or that is what the government calls them. Reverse Mortgages have proven to be a godsend for some people who are cash poor and real estate rich. A Reverse Mortgage provides supplemental income to a homeowner age 62 or older. There are restrictions with Reverse Mortgages. You have to live in the home and it must be your personal residence. You cannot do this with houses that you want to flip.

A lot of attorneys, accountants and advisors do not like Reverse Mortgages, because the homeowner has to pay back the Reverse Mortgage, so it is a liability that grows with interest. In addition, there are normally high closing costs to the transaction, sometimes as high as four percent.

ADVANCED PLANNING USES OF A REVERSE MORTGAGE

There are smart ways to use the Reverse Mortgage to a client's advantage. One of those ways is to take a Reverse Mortgage Line of Credit. You basically receive a checkbook that you can access as needed. You have closing costs, but if you do not ever write a check, then you are not depleting the value of your home. This strategy makes sense for emergency purposes. If a long-term care need arises in the future, then you have ready access to funds immediately. This is part of a little something called financial planning. You have heard of that, haven't you?

Another more exciting use of the Reverse Mortgage Line of Credit is to access the funds to convert your IRA to a Roth IRA. Here is a source of funds that you can use that does not take anything out of your current cash flow. You pay the taxes on the IRA conversion with the Reverse Mortgage Line of Credit. After you do this, 100% of your IRA is now a tax-free Roth IRA. After five years, you can take a withdrawal from your tax free Roth IRA and pay back the Reverse Mortgage Line of Credit. The benefits for you are your house is restored to full value, you have no more required minimum distributions, and you have access to tax free withdrawals from your Roth. In addition, if you do not want to pay it back, then you do not have to pay it back. It will get paid back, though, one way or another.

There is no disputing that using funds outside the IRA is the best way to pay the taxes. If we think taxes are going up, then why wouldn't we eliminate the future tax liability of our IRA? We should. It is the smart thing to do.

The HECM Purchase Program

On January 1, 2009, we have a new option to *buy* property. It is called a HECM Purchase Program, or more commonly known as a Reverse Mortgage Purchase Program. This is going to help people sell their homes.

Here is an example of how this works:

Let us say you wanted to buy a $350,000 home and you are 62 years old or older. You can buy this home free and clear for approximately $123,000. There is a Reverse Mortgage on the difference between the $350,000 and the $123,000. These funds are not paid to you, but rather are used to pay off the house.

For Example:

Home Selling Price = $350,000
Reverse Mortgage paid to the Owner (Seller of the property) = $227,000
Reverse Mortgage payment owed at Buyer's death or sale of the home = $227,000
Buyer puts down payment of $123,000.

The result is that the Seller receives $350,000 ($227,000 because of the Reverse Mortgage Purchase, which is paid back by the Buyer at death or sale of the house, plus the $123,000 down payment.)

In my opinion, this HECM Purchase Program is going to be big. I promise you that I will be talking about it to the people that I work with. The requirements are that you have to be 62 or older or turning 62 within 6 months. In addition, it has to be a home less than $417,000 and it has to be your personal residence that you are purchasing. Further, you have to live in it. How do you like them apples?

DIVORCE PLANNING

Like or not people get divorced. I especially hate to see it when it is among older people. Personally, I think you should try to work it out, but divorce happens nevertheless. In this example, I am assuming that this couple has investment assets in addition to their home.

You can use this Reverse Mortgage purchase option in divorce situations. If you have a home and you are getting divorced, then you have to split it, which means selling it. Alternatively, someone gets the money and the other spouse gets the house. The problem with this is the house is not liquid. It could take a year or more to sell the house. Also, it creates a major problem if you do not have money for upkeep. This is not a workable solution where one spouse gets the house and the other gets the money. Ask anyone who has been through it. They will tell you.

There is a better way, however. Let us assume that husband and wife have a $350,000 home that they have paid off and now they are getting a divorce. The husband in this situation is moving out with his twenty years younger girlfriend who only cares about his money. Sorry, I got a little off track there. Men are pigs you know.

Instead of being forced to sell the home, (think today's housing market) they take out a Reverse Mortgage on the existing home for $227,000. The $227,000 is split 50/50 and half of it goes to the husband. He takes his half and he goes and buys a new $350,000 home. The wife is able to keep her home with no house payments and she gets 50% of the $227,000. She has a home and $113,500 cash.

The husband can put down $123,000 on the $350,000 home and take a Reverse Mortgage purchase to pay the seller the difference. Now, the husband has a $350,000 home with no payments.

After these transactions, it is much easier to split assets. It works for both parties. Tell your friends who are in the unfortunate position of getting a divorce. You heard it here first.

HOME EQUITY LINE OF CREDIT

Everyone should have a Home Equity Line of Credit. Most often, there is minimal to no cost to obtain one. There are three ideas that I like for the HELOC. The first and most obvious one is for emergency fund access. In the case of an emergency, like sudden and unexpected health issues, death of a loved one and the expenses that go with that or the loss of your job.

If one of your family members has to go into a hospital, then there could be a loss of income for a time. Perhaps, you may lose some income, because you have to be by their hospital bedside. Having access to those HELOC funds is smart and part of the financial planning process.

God forbid, one of your family members passes away. The funeral home wants their money and most times, they want it in advance of doing the funeral. The HELOC will give you access to funds to help you in this situation.

What if you lost your job or if your company gave you the option to transfer to another city or state? How would you pay for the duplicate expenses? You may be in a situation with no job and no income. The HELOC will allow you time to find a job. If you have been transferred, you may need a year or more to sell your house. That means duplicate living expenses, but the HELOC will help you through it.

IRA Conversion with a HELOC

The best use of the HELOC is to convert your IRA to a Roth IRA. Get an Interest Only HELOC for this purpose. You write a check from your HELOC to pay the taxes on your IRA conversion to a Roth IRA. Then again, after five years, you take a tax-free withdrawal from the Roth IRA to pay off the HELOC. Sweet!

Okay, if taxes are going up, doesn't it make sense to pay the taxes now, or would you rather wait until your IRA doubles and pay twice as much in taxes or more? By utilizing this strategy, you will be converting your IRA for less than 10% in most cases. That is much better than 33% for you folks in Rio Linda.

Pay off Your House Early

Another neat idea for using your HELOC is to pay off your house. What you can do is pay off your house in a significantly shorter time period. It takes discipline to do this. The best scenario is to have a checking account and your HELOC at the same bank with 24/7 online account access. The reason this is needed is that it will make it easier to do this strategy.

How it works is by depositing your monthly income into your HELOC. You take $10,000 and pay on the principal of your mortgage. Then, you pay all of your monthly expenses via your HELOC's free check writing. You can do this manually if you like, but it is much easier with online banking.

Rick Johnson

You can routinely transfer direct-deposited income from your checking directly into your HELOC. Then, when you need to pay bills, you can move it back into the checking account where your bills are paid. There is a discipline effect to this and you do have to stay on top of this, but if you follow this approach, then you will significantly shorten the time that your mortgage is outstanding. The plan is to deposit income instantly into the HELOC and only pay bills once or twice a month.

Here is a table explaining this concept:

Date	Activity	Amount	HELOC Balance	Available Credit
2/1/2008	First Mortgage Reduction	-$10,000.00	$10,000.00	$15,000.00
2/15/2008	Income Deposit	$2,500.00	$7,533.90	$17,466.10
2/28/2008	Income Deposit	$2,500.00	$5,059.44	$19,940.56
3/1/2008	Monthly Bills	-$2,820.45	$7,879.89	$17,120.11
3/15/2008	Income Deposit	$2,500.00	$5,406.61	$19,593.39
3/30/2008	Income Deposit	$2,500.00	$2,924.94	$22,075.06
4/1/2008	Monthly Bills	-$2,820.45	$5,745.39	$19,254.61
4/15/2008	Income Deposit	$2,500.00	$3,264.87	$21,735.13
05/01/2008	Income Deposit	$2,500.00	$1,108.58	$23,891.42
05/01/2008	Monthly Bills	-$2,820.45	$3,596.39	$21,403.61
05/15/2008	Income Deposit	$2,500.00	$-1,387.66	$26,387.66

In this table, we borrowed $25,000 from our HELOC, but we only accessed $10,000. We paid $10,000 on the first mortgage. Then, we implemented the strategy. We deposited our income directly back into the HELOC. When it became time to pay bills, we paid bills out of the HELOC. We repeated this process until as you can see at the end, we have built our $25,000 line of credit back up. It grew from $15,000 available credit back up to $26,387.66 after a few months.

What you will see happen is that your HELOC $10,000 balance will be paid off quickly. In most cases in just a few months, it is paid off. Then, you take another $10,000 out and repeat the process. Your mortgage will be gone before you know it. You only need a $10,000 line of credit to accomplish this, so do not worry if the bank will only give you a small open line of credit. You are now smarter than they know and have a plan to accomplish. By the way, there is no need to tell your banker about this. They may not like it if you tell them.

Pay off Credit Cards Early

When the IRS took away the deduction for credit card interest, people were told to take out a HELOC and pay off the credit cards. This would give you a tax deduction from the HELOC. You have outsmarted the IRS! However, the only problem was that you moved your debt from one pocket to the other *without paying it off.*

Now, I want you to think about the idea that I just described above using the HELOC to pay down the principal on your mortgage. Instead of paying down your mortgage, I want you to substitute your credit card debt. Deposit your income every month into your HELOC, and then pay your bills once or twice a month. Guess what? Your HELOC balance will grow back to its original credit amount and your credit card debt will be gone in a few months.

Theoretically, you can do this strategy with any kind of debt as long as you have a home equity line of credit balance available. You are getting smarter and smarter, aren't you? It is not that important to have a large amount for a HELOC. You should be able to do this with as little as $10,000 or even $5,000.

ARM's & Negative Amortization Mortgages

I will keep this section short and sweet. The only reason to use ARM's and Negative Amortization Mortgages is to keep the payments low for a very short time and you know that you will be selling the property soon, or your credit is good enough to refinance later at more long term rates. Otherwise, ARM's and Negative Amortization Mortgages will do nothing but put you in precarious position where you will lose your house. This is the reason the economy is in the mess it is in now. People bought houses way out of their price range and bought them with these types of mortgage instruments. They all blew up and here we are in the mother of all housing slumps.

Stay far away from these exotic mortgages. They will create all kinds of problems for you, if you do not watch out.

Retirement Planning

Retirement planning advice or lack of it is the Crime of the Century. There has been a complete disregard for ongoing employee education with regard to 401(k), 403(b) and 457 plans.

Several years ago, the employers of this nation passed on the responsibility of taking care of their employee's pensions to their employees in the form of these plans, primarily the 401(k). However, most companies have done a poor job of offering solid choices in financial planning advice to their employees. As a result, employees have had to fend for themselves.

Most people's investment knowledge is woefully inadequate. Believe me, studying investment alternatives is a full time job and then some. I am sure that you have heard people talking about their 101(k) that used to be a 401(k). That is my proof of the Crime of the Century.

Let me get this straight. An American employee is supposed to put in a 40-hour workweek, come home and worry about fixing dinner, helping the kids with their homework, pay the bills, exercise, spend a little time with their significant other, and then knows what to do with their 401(k) investments? No thanks. That dog won't hunt.

Because of our busy lives, we make a decision to invest our 401(k) at enrollment time based on what some financial services person advised us to do. Typically, this so-called advice is 25% in this, 25% in that, and so on. During enrollment, we just do not get good investment counseling. I have never seen a beautifully diversified 401(k) plan. That is right. I said never. Even my own wife's 401(k) has awful investment options. It is difficult to properly diversify a 401(k) if you do not have enough investment choices. This is the case with my wife's 401(k). There is not enough investment choices. I am sure that there are plenty of other 401(k)'s in the same predicament.

There may be a beautifully diversified 401(k) out there, but I have yet to see it. All I see is horror stories. In other words, there are too many poorly invested retirement plans and too many poor investment choices in retirement plans.

To make matters worse, we usually have no say so over our investment choices. We are typically limited to a set of funds, (some of which we cannot even find in the newspaper) which are mediocre at best. Then, the financial services salesperson tells us that we really should be making the maximum contribution to our 401(k). Most of us are a little skeptical, because we know this person does not have our best interest at heart. All they care about is getting us to invest, so they will make more money in commissions or fees.

We are sold on the fact that we have to do something and at least the company is matching something of what I put in. Therefore, this is in effect free money to us. Even if our performance is mediocre, we are still better off. So, what do we do? We contribute up to the amount that our company contributes. You may be thinking if they are only matching on the first 5%, then I am only putting in 5% into my 401(k). This is absolutely the wrong way to look at this.

Many of our country's 401(k) plans have our company stock in them. This can be good and this can be bad. It all depends on the company. Generally, the more you concentrate your 401(k) in your company stock, the more you live and die by what your company stock does.

As you get closer to retirement age, it is probably a real good idea to divest yourself of your company stock and move your money into safer, fixed income investments. If you fail to do this, you will not be retiring anytime soon. You will be working several more years hoping your company stock comes back up. There is a lot of "hope" in investing these days, isn't there?

You will see corporate America cutting back on matching 401(k) contributions now. There are several companies who have already made the cutbacks.

CAN YOU SAY LAWSUIT?

There is a problem between employees and their employers over their 401(k)'s. It appears that there is a gap between the high-ranking employers and their staff. The issue revolves around the employer who goes out and hires a financial advisor to help him manage his or her 401(k). In turn, the poor rank and file employees have to fend for themselves. The problem is that this causes the employer's 401(k) performance to significantly outperform the employee's performance. ERISA attorneys are chomping at the bit at the potential for litigation here.

So, what is a hard working American employer to do? First, you need to quit doing what everybody else is doing. Your company 401(k) needs to be with a firm that assumes most of the fiduciary responsibility. Secondarily, you need to make sure that your plan is age based whereby everyone in the same age group receives the same return. Just because you own the place does not mean that you deserve a better return than your employees do.

Here is a common erroneous practice involving corporate America and their 401(k) plans. The highly compensated executives have an option to carve out their 401(k) dollars from the poor mutual fund choices. The rank and file employees are stuck with those lousy fund choices. These highly compensated executives can have a pension trust account at their favorite financial advisor's firm and buy whatever investments they want to. For some reason, the lowly rank and file employees do not have that option or are not educated by the employers as to how to take advantage of it. Therefore, Houston, we have a problem. This is a lawsuit waiting to happen.

RETIREMENT PLAN MISTAKES

It is hard not to make mistakes with regard to your retirement plan these days. We do not have good choices concerning our 401(k), 403(b) and 457 these days. Most of these plans limit us to a small selection of funds. We tend to make poor investment decisions with our retirement plans. If we work for a major company, we feel obligated to buy our company's stock. Typically, we over allocate dollars to our company stock, then our company stock goes from bad to worse and we get crushed.

Most of the mistakes we make with our retirement plans are over allocation of the wrong asset classes. If we are making the decisions on our own, then we review the investment performance to make our decision. Remember how meaningless I said investment performance is? Nevertheless, we scour the past performance information given to us by the retirement plan sponsor and end up choosing a mix of funds based on performance. Then, after we lose money, we cannot understand what just happened? We picked the best available performing funds. Why didn't this work?

It does not work for the same reasons that I wrote about earlier. That past performance was good for that period, but it is not good for the future. You have to make investment selections based on the future, not the past. In a bear market, it is a little easier decision. Think about loading up on stocks in early 2009. How many of you are brave enough to do that? Not too many of you I would presume.

When it is a bull market however, you have no qualms about jumping head first into the stock market. You perceive that there is less risk when it is a bull market. You perceive that there is more risk when it is a bear market.

In reality, the opposites are true. If you have a lump sum of cash to invest after the stock market has dropped over 40%, then the odds are over time you should do well.

Conversely, if the stock market has gone up over 40% recently, then by reducing your exposure to stocks should benefit you.

Both of these concepts are polar opposites of what most people do. Most people buy high and sell low. This stuff is not easy. Personally, you need a professional who thinks this way and is not afraid to go to cash.

SOLUTIONS

The other side of the coin that nobody bothers to tell you about is the tax consequences of withdrawals from your 401(k), 403(b), 457 plans or IRA account.

Every financial advisor and again I use this term very loosely, tells you to try to do everything you can to maximize your 401(k) and IRA contributions. Putting away the maximum each year will grow like a weed for you, they tell you. What they fail to explain to you are the tax consequences.

If we think that taxes may go up in the future, then why would we wait until we are 70 ½ before we start pulling money out of our IRA's and 401(k)'s? Does this really make sense?

Of course, the objection to this way of thinking is that we would have to pay taxes if we pulled money out. Therefore, what everyone in America does is wait until they are 70 ½ to start their taxable withdrawals. The cows are headed to the slaughterhouse and they do not even know it.

What if there was a way to convert your IRA and 401(k) accounts today with little or no impact on your cash flow? What if you could do it for less than 10% in taxes instead of 25%, 28%, 33% or 35%? How is this possible?

Several successful authors have written books on this subject. The straightest shooter on the subject that I have read is written by Roccy DeFrancesco, JD, CWPP™, CAPP™, MMB™". *The Home Equity Management Guidebook* is the name of it. This book is a little hard to follow for most folks, because of the technical jargon, but he gives it to you straight. Most of these authors agree that the equity in your home earns a zero rate of return. In most cases, you can withdraw up to $100,000 in home equity and get a tax deduction for doing so. You take the $100,000 and pay the income taxes on your IRA or 401(k) conversion to a Roth IRA. If you do your algebra equation on that then you would find that you could convert around $300,000 of your IRA or 401(k) assuming you are in a 33% tax bracket.

Yes Rick, but you would have to pay the mortgage. True, but the mortgage is simple interest. After you paid the taxes with the home equity loan, then you would have a $300,000 Roth IRA. After 5 years, your Roth should have easily grown with compound interest to around $400,000, assuming of course that you use a conservative financial advisor like me. Then, at this point, you can take tax-free withdrawals from your Roth IRA. In the sixth year, you simply pay off your $100,000 home equity loan. Now you have a totally tax free Roth IRA.

You get a tax deduction assuming you itemize (Schedule A – IRS form) and you have not already borrowed everything out of your house. Let us say you have to pay 8% on the $100,000 loan. This is $8,000, but in a 33% bracket, it actually becomes roughly 5.33%, or $5,330. Take $5,330 times 5 years and you have $26,650. Then, divide $300,000 by $26,650 and you get 8.88%. It cost you 8.88% to convert $300,000 of your IRA or 401(k) into a tax free Roth IRA. That is 8.88% instead of 33% for you folks in Rio Linda as Rush Limbaugh likes to say.

Here is the overriding point on this strategy. If you use money that is earning interest, then you lose the interest that you would have earned on those funds. Therefore, you would have to add that lost interest on top of your borrowing costs. It does not make sense and neither does taking it out of the IRA or 401(k) to pay the taxes. However, if you leverage dollars that are currently earning a zero rate of return, then it makes a whole lot more sense.

The question becomes though, how I am going to pay for the loan. The tough question is how would you rather pay taxes on a $300,000 IRA? Would you prefer to pay it all at once which would ordinarily cost you $100,000 out of your other investments? Alternatively, would you rather pay $26,650 spread out over 5 years? You tell me. If you take $100,000 out of your other investments, then you are taking $100,000 off the table and lose the interest on that money. If you borrow $100,000 out of your house, you are not losing any interest on it.

Another way to do this may be with a Reverse Mortgage Line of Credit that I discussed earlier. Did you know that you could get a Line of Credit Reverse Mortgage and only take out what you need? Take the lump sum

Reverse Mortgage proceeds needed and pay the taxes on your IRA to Roth IRA conversion. After five years, pay off the Reverse Mortgage from the tax-free Roth. Good thinking Watson.

Assuming Congress does not do anything to jeopardize things, everyone should be able to convert their IRA's and 401(k)'s to Roth IRA's in the year 2010. There is nothing stopping you from spreading it out over an even longer time period like 10 years. The way it stands now, you will be able to spread the taxes out over two years if you convert in the year 2010.

A NEW WAY OF THINKING – A TAX FREE RETIREMENT

Now you must remember to think differently from the herd. After all, the baton has been handed off to you. So, do not drop it as they did in China at the Olympics!

Does it really make sense to keep funding your IRA or 401(k), especially since we all believe taxes may go higher in the future? If we delay the inevitable, are we not increasing our tax liability every year? It makes better sense to pay the taxes now.

I have met people with a million dollars in their IRA accounts. They are proud that they have accumulated those funds. The only trouble is they do not really have a million dollars. If they do like everyone else in America and wait until age 70 ½ to pull the required minimum distribution out each year, then they will likely pay a ton more in taxes over their life expectancy.

After they pass away, what do you think the kids will do? They will want that money, especially, if they are not educated enough in how to properly structure their share of the IRA. They will most likely squander most of it away to taxes. Nothing happens automatically here folks. You have to have a knowledgeable professional who knows how to stretch an IRA properly. They must know how to get the funds to an Inherited IRA. They must know whether to take distributions because of the deceased person being over 70 ½ at death or under 70 ½ at death. They must know the deadlines to take the required minimum distributions for the beneficiaries.

Many people think that they are supposed to take their required minimum distributions by April 15th of the year following when they turn 70 ½, but in fact it is April 1st, not April 15th. It certainly helps to also know what to do if there is a failure to take the required minimum distribution. The penalty for failure to take these distributions out properly is 50% of the required distribution.

We met a client once whose mother had died and he had setup the Inherited IRA about eight years ago. The only problem was that he never took out the required minimum distribution in any of those eight years. Guess what, he had a 50% penalty for each of the years that he missed. He did not get much of that Inherited IRA. The IRS got it. Is this what you want to happen to your adult children? You had better work with a professional who knows these rules.

Think about what it would be like to use your home equity or a Reverse Mortgage and convert a portion of your IRA or 401(k) to a tax-free Roth IRA account. You would never have to pay taxes on the Roth IRA from that point on. No required minimum distributions ever.

The Roth 403(b) is also available for schoolteachers, professors, medical professionals and other groups.

Many people who come and see us think that they cannot convert their IRA to a Roth. As long as your Adjusted Gross Income is under $100,000 then you can. In 2010, anyone can convert because they are removing this $100,000 AGI limitation. It is a good idea to begin planning now. Further, there are ways to reduce your AGI in order to convert to a Roth IRA today.

What do you do if you are one of the unfortunate Americans who do not have a Roth 401(k)? You make the full contributions to your Roth IRA every year. Put it away each year and act like you never had those funds in the first place. Better yet, every time you receive a raise in pay, bump up your contribution a little more, until you max out.

The Roth 401(k), the Roth 403(b) and the Roth IRA will all have their maximum limit for contributions raised for the next few years. Okay, here is another quiz question for you. Did you know there was such a thing as a Roth 403(b)? That is what I thought!

Putting money into these Roth accounts are without a doubt one of the best things that you could ever do for yourself and your family. Do not make the mistake of beating yourself up with regard to how to invest it. After all, in year one if, you make 20% and all you put in is $1,000, then your account will only grow $200. Is this really going to make you dance in the streets? The best thing that could happen to you is your account does not make a dime for the first 5 years. Just sock it away. After several years of maximizing your contributions, you will be pleasantly surprised to see how it jumps up when you do make a good return.

If you are self-employed, then you may utilize a more recent option to start an Individual Roth 401(k). The best thing to do is to hire a professional to help you figure out what might be the best fit for your business. The point is that being a self-employed businessperson will allow you great flexibility in saving for retirement with after-tax dollars.

Build your emergency cash position first. Then pay off your debt. After you have accomplished these two things, then you can begin to think about saving and investing for growth. Save all that you can in your Roth retirement plans. If you are lucky enough to have additional funds left over, then continue to invest on a regular basis month in and month out. Do not make the mistake of believing the lump sum that you have accumulated today is all that you need to make it the rest of your life.

Do not listen to financial advisors and CPA's who tell you to make the most of pre-tax IRA and 401(k) contributions. All they are doing is creating a big retirement plan for the IRS, not you. Tax-free is a big, big difference over taxable. Instead, go with the Roth all the way. You do not have to walk into the tax slaughterhouse. You can do something about it today. Now you know.

RETIREMENT INCOME PLANNING

When we are lucky enough to make it to retirement with our stash of retirement funds, then we discover the ugly truth about retirement. We have lost all of deductions. Most often, we have worked all of our life to pay off our house, so we do not have that tax write off. Our kids are long gone and we have no deduction for them anymore. In addition, since we are no longer working, we have lost our IRA or retirement plan tax deduction. If you are lucky enough to have a pension check coming in each month, then you know that that is 100% taxable to you. When our Social Security check arrives, we find that we have to pay taxes on it too. In most cases, 85% of it is taxed.

Now that we are retired, we find ourselves in the predicament of having to pay more taxes than we are used to paying. Most people shrug their shoulders and assume this is the way it is and there is nothing that can be done.

MISTAKES

Perhaps the biggest mistake that I see from people is that they continue the same investment mix that they had prior to retirement. In other words, they have investments that are in taxable mutual funds, taxable bonds and CD's. In their IRA accounts, they have not made any changes to the investment mix. It still has a large slant towards stocks or stock mutual funds. They are taking way too much risk in their IRA accounts.

When you are retired, you have to make changes to your investment mix. You cannot continue to accept the inherent risk associated with the stock market. You need to make decisions to protect your principal.

Imagine that you retired in the spring of 2008 and you left your $1,000,000 investment portfolio invested without any meaningful changes. You assumed that you were going to pull 5% or $50,000 out each year. While the market was declining, your financial advisor was telling you to hold on. Now, fast forward to the end of 2008. Your $1,000,000 is now worth $600,000. You are down 40%. Believe me, there are many people in America that this actually happened to in 2008.

Do you think that this person would be able to pull $50,000 per year out as planned? Now, that represents 8.33% as the withdrawal rate. Money market rates are around 1% or less. How is this person going to get 8.33% for a return? They are not. In fact, I would venture to say that even a 5% withdrawal rate would be a big stretch.

Could this all have been avoided if they moved their portfolio to protect their principal? It would have made a big difference in their lifestyle in retirement. You have to make changes in your portfolio as you reach retirement. You cannot just let it ride.

SOLUTIONS

Taxation is key in retirement. The goal should be to minimize taxable income. One way to do this is by dividing your assets into three pools or buckets of money. I want to explain the concept by using a combination of a single premium immediate annuity and a couple of tax deferred annuities.

What most people do not understand about annuities is how to structure them in a portfolio. This approach has been called many different things. It has been called buckets, laddering, pools of money and I am sure a host of other things. In reality, it is the split annuity concept. The strategy is to have a portion pay a guaranteed income and defer another larger portion that grows back to your original principal. The guaranteed portion is called a (SPIA) single premium immediate annuity and there is very little of it that is subject to taxes. The reason for this is that it is mostly a return of principal. You want your SPIA to be paid back in the shortest time period available, which is five years.

If your principal is returned to you over a five-year period, then there are very little taxes. Why would you want to do this? Let us assume that you have $1,000,000 to invest. If you invested it in mutual funds, you would pay taxes on the interest, dividends and capital gains. You would pay taxes on the interest and dividends over the five-year period and if you sold it all at the end, then you would pay capital gains on the growth. Assuming of course, the stock market went up. I shudder to think about losing 40% of your original principal. I know that has to hurt.

With the SPIA 5 year period certain payout, you are primarily getting your principal returned to you which you can use for income. The idea behind this strategy is that it is taxed very little. Of course, you do not put all your money in an immediate annuity. The idea is to put a larger balance in deferred growth annuities that grow preferably in five or 10-year increments.

When the 5 year SPIA is depleted, then you make the 5 year growth annuity an SPIA with a 5 year period certain payout. Then, after 10 years, you make the 10 year growth annuity a SPIA with a 5 year period certain payout. You can repeat this process indefinitely. All along, you have minimized taxes because you are living off an immediate annuity for income. Class, what is the taxation of an immediate annuity? Very little thank you.

There is a calculation to this strategy. A rough calculation would say that you put 28% in the SPIA, 22% in the 5-year growth annuity and 50% in the 10-year growth annuity. With a $1,000,000 original investment, you would put $280,000 in the SPIA, $220,000 in the 5-year growth annuity and $500,000 in the 10-year growth annuity. The $280,000 is paid back to you over five years, so an easy calculation would tell you that it would provide you with $56,000 plus a little interest annually. Stop the presses! $56,000 divided by $1,000,000 is how much? That is a 5.6% income generated on your $1,000,000 that is guaranteed for the next five years.

The second leg or the five-year growth annuity would need to earn 4.94% for those five years. If it earned that, then it would grow back to the $280,000 to continue the $56,000 per year for another 5 years. All the while, the ten-year growth annuity is still growing.

The third leg or the ten-year growth annuity would need to earn 7.18% for it to grow back to $1,000,000. You would think over time that you would be able to do this. Of course if you thought this was a stretch to achieve, then you could decide not to spend some of the $56,000 that you receive it year. After all, it is your principal being returned to you. Or, as an alternative, you could have one SPIA providing income for five years and one five-year growth annuity growing back to the original principal. It would be a math calculation to figure out how much to put into each. The 10-year growth annuity is only necessary if you have a 10-year time horizon.

Alternatively, you could also lengthen it by going to a 15 or 20 year time period. It depends on your needs.

The advantage of this strategy is that you are receiving primarily your principal as income each year. There are no taxes due on principal. Therefore, instead of living off dividends and interest, which are taxable each year, you would utilize this principal based strategy. It makes sense because it is tax efficient.

It is also possible to actually reduce your taxable Social Security income utilizing this strategy. Consider if you were taking 5.6% out in taxable dividends and interest. This means that you were adding $56,000 to your Adjusted Gross Income. If however you utilized this split annuity concept, then the $56,000 paid to you would actually reduce your taxable income by $56,000. That may actually put you in a lower tax bracket, thus saving you taxes. Another advantage would be that it might also lower your taxable income to the point where you are only taxed on 50% of your Social Security income instead of 85%. Or maybe, it might lower your income to where you do not pay any taxes on your Social Security income.

Do you see? Annuities have a good side to them.

Tax Planning

In taxable accounts, the income earned through dividends, interest and capital gains are taxed. This is how most people invest their taxable monies. They buy things that spin off interest, dividends and capital gains. The problem here is that taxes are due every year. If you have to pay taxes each year, then that depletes the growth of your assets.

If you have held assets for more than one year, then you would be subject to capital gains taxes if you were to sell them. In the year 2011, if no new legislation is enacted, there will be an increase back to the 20% capital gains tax rate.

Mistakes

The most common tax-planning mistake is to pay tax on income that you do not need. Other mistakes involve missed itemized deductions and missed tax credits.

In my opinion, I believe it is sound advice to get a second opinion on your tax return. After you have looked at as many tax returns as I have, it is easy to find mistakes. If you never get a second opinion on your tax return, especially if you are the one doing the taxes, then you will never know whether you are doing the right thing.

Did you know that in 2009 and 2010, if your adjusted gross income is under $65,100, then you qualify for the 0% capital gains tax rate? This means that if you have been holding something because you did not want to pay the capital gains taxes on it, then this will allow you to sell without a capital gains tax. Did you know about this? If not, then I just proved to you why you need a second opinion on your tax return.

Down with taxes and up with income. This is what most everyone in America does. They invest in things that pay interest, dividends and capital gains. This is really about all there is to invest in or so you think. Let us assume that you have $500,000 to invest. You go to what you believe to be is a competent financial advisor and they build a portfolio of investments for you. In this portfolio, you have money market funds, equity mutual funds, bond mutual funds and stocks. The money market funds pay interest income. The bond mutual funds pay dividend income. The equity mutual funds and stocks also pay dividends. The equity mutual funds spin off uncontrollable capital gains based on the whims of other investors, as I mentioned earlier. The stocks are subject to capital gains when you sell them.

The only thing that you can control here is the capital gains from the stocks. Everything else is paid to you because of what you invested in. The result is that taxes are due regardless whether or not you reinvested the interest, dividends and capital gains from the equity mutual funds.

Most people who buy mutual funds blindly do so because everyone else and their brother do the same thing. They just accept the fact that they spin off taxes that they cannot control. They think that this is the only alternative. It is not the only alternative.

Let me explain via an example. Assume that you put $500,000 in a portfolio of mutual funds in November of a given year. Within one month, your portfolio is going to spin off a bunch of short-term capital gains, long-term capital gains and dividends that you will have to pay taxes on. Right out of the gate, you are hit with a tax bill. This is not smart.

Instead, assume that you put the $500,000 in a portfolio of Exchange Traded Funds. The Exchange Traded Funds rarely spin off capital gains. The only thing that you are taxed on is the minimal dividends of the fixed income Exchange Traded Funds. The principal amount invested in Exchange Traded Funds are tax deferred until you sell them.

This is what you need to know about how ETF's work. Suppose that I am a pension fund, I have $50,000,000 invested in an S&P 500 ETF, and I want to sell it. The ETF fund can hand back the stocks inside the S&P 500 ETF to the pension fund, instead of being forced to sell the stocks, as mutual funds have to do. This saves you money if you own this S&P 500 ETF. Your holdings are not adversely affected by the whims of some big pension plan. This is why they are tax efficient.

Compared to a portfolio of taxable mutual funds, you would save a tremendous amount in taxes, not to mention the mutual funds fees. When you add in the compounding effect of saving taxes and expenses, then you will be way ahead of a mutual fund portfolio. In the same way that you have been taught to buy mutual funds, most financial advisors have been told to sell them.

You have to make a change away from mutual funds. Listen to me. They are bad for you from an expenses and tax perspective. Why do you think Vanguard Mutual Funds now has Exchange Traded Funds (ETF's)? It is the future my friend. You will see more and more mutual fund companies get into the ETF business.

LONG TERM CARE PLANNING

Long-term care in and of itself is a challenge. Nursing homes used to be one of the main options, but today they are looked at as a last result. Most people do not want to go into a nursing home. Instead, they try to get family members to take care of them as long as possible. The smart ones buy long-term care insurance in one form or another.

Long-term care insurance can be expensive. Most people assume they will not need long term care insurance, because they think they will just keel over and die. In reality, this is not true. I know that I am generalizing here, but many people will go through three or four years and sometimes more of long term care needs.

MISTAKES

Of course, the number one answer with regard to long-term care is to assume that it is not needed. So, people just choose to self insure or do without it. Neither of those are good decisions.

SOLUTIONS

What if you could find long-term care insurance that would take care of long-term care expenses on an as needed basis?

There are actually two options available that fit this bill. These options are hybrid products. One is a hybrid single premium life insurance policy with a long-term care rider. The other alternative is a fixed annuity with a long-term care rider. Let us discuss the hybrid single premium life policy with the LTC rider. This product works in the following manner. If you put $50,000 into the policy, you would have an immediate death benefit and LTC benefit amount. The death benefit depends on the age of the insured, but hypothetically may be twice the amount of the premium. In this case, it may provide $100,000 of death benefit.

If LTC expenses arise, then the policy will pay a monthly benefit for qualified LTC expenses, which may last for 6 years. Again, I am simplifying the matter, but let us assume it pays $4,000 a month for qualified LTC expenses for a maximum of 6 years. The $4,000 per month is tax free if qualified for LTC expenses. The payment is considered an advance of the death benefit for tax purposes.

You would need to qualify for this policy medically. In other words, you need to be insurable. You can have some minor health problems and still get one of these policies, but nothing major can be wrong with you.

The advantage of the single premium life insurance policy with long-term care rider is that if you do not need money for long-term care expenses, then you have not wasted any money on LTC insurance premiums. This type of policy has a cash value if you live and it has a death benefit if you died suddenly. It makes more sense. The only drawback is if you have a prolonged LTC illness that is more than the benefit period. In other words, if you need long term care for more than six years, then the traditional type of LTC insurance may be more appropriate. The problem is that nobody really knows the day or the hour.

You may be wondering what if you currently have health problems or cannot qualify for traditional LTC insurance or this hybrid single premium life insurance with LTC rider. If this is your predicament, then there is good news. The hybrid fixed annuity with LTC rider is your answer.

In this example, if you put in $50,000, then you have $50,000 plus interest earnings that can be paid out in qualified LTC expenses. In effect, the $50,000 that you put into this hybrid annuity acts as sinking fund if you need money for LTC. If you do not ever need LTC, then it acts as a fixed annuity. Again, you have not wasted premiums on traditional LTC insurance that you may never need.

You might be thinking that this is no different than if you were self-insuring, but you would be wrong. A hybrid annuity with a LTC rider starting January 1, 2010 will allow *tax-free* LTC benefit payments for qualified LTC expenses. You have to understand that a regular annuity has a cost basis. You are taxed at ordinary income rates on the earnings. With the hybrid annuity however, the benefits for qualified LTC expenses are *tax-free*.

If you are self insured with a regular annuity and used the proceeds for LTC expenses, then you would pay taxes on every withdrawal based on how much is cost basis and how much is earnings. So, if you $50,000 self-insured annuity grew to $100,000, then you would owe taxes on half of it.

With the hybrid annuity with LTC rider, if it were to grow to $100,000 and you needed LTC expense money, then you can access it *tax-free*. This is a big difference. In my mind, you should not have an annuity going forward unless it has a LTC rider on it that pays a monthly benefit for qualified LTC expenses. Or, it is even better if you go with the hybrid single premium life insurance policy with a LTC rider. You get the death benefit as a bonus.

If you can qualify medically, then you go with the hybrid single premium life with LTC rider. If you cannot qualify medically, then you go with the hybrid annuity with LTC rider.

DISABILITY PLANNING

The most obvious challenge with regard to disability planning is not having disability insurance to protect your income. Of course, this applies to people who are still working and are in the age qualification range for disability income insurance policies.

If you become disabled, then it will be extremely difficult to make ends meet unless you have sufficient resources elsewhere. This is even more so if you are a business owner and you have several people depending on you. Perhaps, you are a partner in a law firm and you are the primary rainmaker. If something happens to you, then the whole law firm is at risk without disability insurance.

Suppose you are in the medical field. The same would be true. If a disabling injury happened to you, then your medical practice would be at risk without the proper disability coverage.

Business owners are the ones who make the most mistakes with regard to disability insurance coverage. Business overhead expense insurance will cover all the expenses of your business except your own salary. This BOE coverage is relatively inexpensive. It will shock you how inexpensive it is. You should look into it, believe me.

In addition, if you are in partnership with others, then you should look at Disability Buy-Out Insurance. This is protection against going into business with your partner's spouse. You may be familiar with Buy-Sell agreements that utilize life insurance policies on the partners. Well, with Disability Buy-Out insurance, it rather works the same way, except it covers disability on the partners. This insurance will provide the much-needed funds to buy out your disabled partner's share of the business in case of a permanent disability.

SOLUTIONS

If you are in the professional field, you really should apply for disability insurance while you are in medical school, pharmacy school, engineering school, law school or graduate school. The disability insurance carriers will provide you with reduced premiums while you are still in school. After you are at work full time in your chosen field, then they will adjust the cost according to your income.

If you are a business owner or professional, then make sure you protect your income. In addition, consider Business Overhead Expense insurance and or Disability Buy Out insurance. After all, you do not want to go into business inadvertently with your partner's spouse.

If you are a rank and file employee at a firm that offers disability insurance, then get the most short and long-term disability insurance that you can buy. Typically, it is very inexpensive and offers the protection that you need. Do not skimp on this coverage.

ESTATE PLANNING

The current Estate Tax rates are schedule to go up in 2011 because the minimum taxable estate is scheduled to go back down to $1,000,000. The estate tax rate in 2011 will be 41% for the first dollar over $1,000,000 and can reach 55% at its highest. There is absolutely nothing that needs to be done for this to happen. It is already scheduled due to the sunset provision of the Bush tax cuts.

It is hard to believe, but people in their late sixties and early seventies still do not have their legal documents prepared. I often meet people who have not hired an attorney to draft a will, much less a revocable trust. They risk dying intestate and having the court decide what to do with their assets.

I had a young client who died and named his minor children the beneficiaries of his life insurance policy. This client was divorced and there was a court battle with significant legal fees for the right to be the guardian of the kid's money. The new wife, who was not the kid's mother wanted to control the money. The ex-wife had to hire an attorney and go through a protracted legal battle to gain access to her own children's guardianship. The client who died did not have a will naming a guardian for his children. Therefore, the court had to decide. Unfortunately, there were additional expenses each year until the children reached legal age. An attorney had to be involved and there had to be an accounting every year to the court. All of this could have been avoided with the proper legal documents.

ESTATE SPLITTING

Tons of people make this mistake. They fail to split their estate. What I mean by this is that they put everything in joint name and nothing in their individual names. When one spouse dies, the estate tax exemption is wasted. For 2009, it is $1,455,800 and for people dying in 2010, it is unlimited. It reverts to $348,500 in 2011, which is still a whole lot of money to ignore.

A 2011 example would be where a family has a $2,000,000 estate and they each own $1,000,000 apiece. When one spouse dies, they owe no estate taxes on their portion because they have an exemption for their first $1,000,000 in assets. This saves them estate taxes of $348,500. The $1,000,000 does not go to the surviving spouse at death, but rather to a bypass trust for surviving family members. The bypass trust can be setup to allow the spouse to invade the principal for their health and welfare. In addition, if structured properly, they can receive income from it as long as they live.

Conversely, if they owned everything in joint name, then the $348,500 estate tax savings is lost forever.

LIFE INSURANCE ISSUES

The death benefit of your life insurance is includable in the calculation for estate taxes. This has not been much of concern lately because of the high estate tax exemptions. However, reality will set in again in 2011 when the threshold reverts to $1,000,000. It is easy to artificially inflate your estate for estate tax purposes by owning your own life insurance policies. You really should have your life insurance policies applied for in the name of a life insurance trust that is irrevocable. This removes the value of the death benefit from your estate.

There is a three-year look back rule when you transfer existing life insurance policies into an irrevocable life insurance trust. This means that the IRS will include your existing life insurance policy in your estate tax calculation for the three years after you transfer it to an irrevocable life insurance trust. After that, you are home free and will have removed it from your estate.

SOLUTIONS

I had a friend of mine who was going to get married to a woman who had been married twice before. This woman had won a judgment against her prior husband for alimony for life. That is right. I said alimony for life.

My advice to my friend, since he owned several real estate properties was to do some asset protection planning with domestic irrevocable trusts. I am not a big fan of offshore irrevocable trusts naming some person on an island somewhere the trustee of your assets. I prefer the domestic irrevocable trusts where you name and know the trustee.

Asset protection with domestic irrevocable trusts is similar to not risking everything on one endeavor. What we did was hire an attorney to draft ten separate trusts. We gave each trust a unique name with the name of a city in another state. Then, we hired a separate corporate co-trustee for each trust with a trusted co-trustee who was a friend of the grantor. We put one property into each trust. Each trust was the owner of one property. Therefore, if one trust was sued, there could be no claim against the other properties since they each had separate ownership.

Another critical step was that we had one trust buy the properties, then turn around and sell the properties to the other trusts. So, when the suing attorney goes to find ownership of the properties in the public record, all that they will see is the Wolf trust sold a piece of property to the Lamb trust.

As luck would have it, the marriage did not last long. The famous threat from the ex-wife was that she was going to bust the trusts. I told my friend not to worry. As soon as her attorney figured out that he could not make any money off this on a contingency basis, then he would fade away. Once the attorney figures out that he has to charge the client, then the client does not want to pay a bunch of legal fees. The client thought that she could get the attorney to do it on a contingency, because her ex-husband owned all these properties. In fact, her ex-husband did not own them any more because he had given them away to the trusts. The bottom line was my friend did not lose a dime. He ended up getting half of his ex-wife's property!

Asset protection planning is a good thing. Sometimes it pays to hire a good financial planner like me who knows about advanced asset protection strategies. By the way, the client in this example was a former IRS agent.

ZEROES ARE GOOD

Do you have a large estate with significant estate tax liability? Ordinarily, if you are trying to reduce your taxable estate, then you can start an annual gifting program. This allows $13,000 per beneficiary to be gifted without gift taxes for 2009. In addition, there is a $1,000,000 gift tax exemption per beneficiary that can be utilized. The problem is if you have a larger estate, then you cannot get rid of your assets quick enough with these two strategies.

Enter the Rolling 2 Year Zeroed Out GRAT strategy for a potential solution. With this strategy, you setup intentionally defective grantor trusts for each beneficiary. The grantor pays the taxes on these trusts which means they are not considered a gift. This allows an unlimited amount to be put into the strategy. For example, let us say you have a $20,000,000 estate and you wish to reduce it to a core amount of $3,000,000. This means that you want to give away to family members (in trust) the balance of $17,000,000.

What you do is structure each trust to pay you the grantor, two annual payments based on the IRS 7520 rates. Everything that the GRAT earns over and above this low 7520 rate is effectively given to the beneficiary estate and gift tax-free.

Here are some numbers to further explain the concept. Let us start with one $2,000,000 GRAT as an example.

- $2,000,000 GRAT established.
- Two payments calculated with the 7520 rates.
- Each payment is 52.41% of the principal.
- First year payment is $1,048,200.
- Second year payment is $1,048,200.
- The trust earns an additional $89,600 in interest at the end of the two years. This $89,600 is over and above the amount paid back to the grantor.
- The beneficiary via the trust receives $89,600 gift tax free as opposed to a regular gifting strategy of $13,000.

This Rolling GRAT strategy is repeated every two years. In the years when the trust does not make any money over and above the 7520, the grantor is no worse off. This strategy is repeated until the estate is reduced to the desired core level. It is very critical to zero out the trust. In other words, the grantor must get back their entire contribution plus the 7520 interest. Otherwise, if they left any part of their original contribution in the trust, then it would be a taxable gift.

CHARITABLE PLANNING

I would be neglecting my duties if I did not bring up some neat charitable planning ideas. Do you have an IRA that you are taking your required minimum distributions from each year? Do you need those funds? If not, then consider using them as the premium on a life insurance policy that you leave the death benefit to your favorite charity. This is an easy way to leave a significant sum to your favorite charity.

I can get rid of any estate taxes for anyone by virtue of establishing a Private Foundation as the beneficiary of an estate. If you give all your assets to a charity, then you would owe no estate taxes. A Private Foundation has a requirement that says that 5% must be distributed to a charity each year. In this market environment, that may put the principal at risk. Nevertheless, a Private Foundation must contribute to charitable causes each year. You can put family members on the Board of Trustees and it allows you the opportunity to teach much needed values to your younger family members.

Another alternative is to have a living trust on the husband and a living trust on the wife. When one passes away, their individually owned property is put into a C trust for as long as the surviving spouse lives. Then, when the surviving spouse dies, the first to die spouse's C trust goes to their favorite charity.

Of course, there are Charitable trusts where you can receive the income from your gift as long as you are alive, then when you pass away, the principal goes to the charity. These are called Charitable Remainder Trusts

Alternatively, the converse is true also; you put principal in a trust and give the income to the charity from the principal investment. Then, when you pass away, the principal goes to your beneficiaries. These are called Charitable Lead Trusts.

If you will notice, these ideas require the use of trusts and therefore attorneys. You do not want to do-it-yourself in the charitable planning arena.

Whether you choose any of these concepts, you are receiving an immediate income tax deduction and removing the assets from your estate. The more important reason however is to benefit your favorite charity. After a year like 2008, they need all the help they can get. Go ask your priest, preacher, minister, rabbi, iman or whomever is leading you spiritually, if they need charitable donations right now. I would bet that they would tell you they need charitable donations now more than ever.

Everything you have is because of God's will for you. Do not be naive enough to think that you earned it all by yourself. In my review of people's tax returns, I am amazed to see people with over $2,000,000 and many bountiful blessings who only give a pittance to charity. Every dollar you give in cash, you will receive fifty cents back as a tax deduction. Therefore, if you are giving $5,000 a year, then you must know that it only costs you $2,500 a year to give that $5,000. Now, you should be able to see things differently. If you want to give $5,000 a year, then give $10,000 and you will receive $5,000 back on your tax return against your Adjusted Gross Income. This is how you should make your decisions to contribute to your favorite charities.

REAL ESTATE PLANNING

Here in lies the problem with mortgages. Let us say that you pay extra on your principal each month. Debt gurus are always telling you to pay your house off early. The problem arises when you lose your job, or become disabled. Now what are you going to do? Could you not have used that extra money that you sent to the mortgage lender to tide you over until you found another job?

You cannot rely on the government to help you. A famous quote that seems *apropos* today is from President Ronald Reagan. He said, "The government is not the solution. The government is the problem".

What if you put the extra dollars in a savings account for twelve months instead of sending it to the mortgage company? If you lost your job, at least you could have paid the mortgage for a while until you found another job.

Suppose instead of losing your job, you became sick or disabled. Without disability insurance, you are really in trouble if you plowed extra money into your home. The point here is that putting extra money with the mortgage company is a bad idea. You do not make a dime of interest on it and you cannot access it in an emergency. Yes Rick, but I can get a home equity line of credit. This is certainly not a possibility when you lose your job or become disabled. You had better have your home equity line of credit in place right now and for as much as you can get.

Here are my rules for paying extra on your mortgage. You must have a secure job. Who has a secure job these days? In addition, you must have disability insurance. Most of you do not have disability insurance, do you? Further, you must have an ample supply of emergency funds. Living paycheck to paycheck, are we? Nowadays, a more prudent approach may be

116

to have a year's worth of emergency funds, instead of three to six months. The bottom line is that you should think before you give your money away to the bank. Be smart about it.

Mistakes

The mistake that people make with regard to real estate is the same with stocks. You buy your real estate too high and you sell your real estate too low. When you are buying real property, you really need to slow it down and make a good decision. After all, you are purchasing a relatively illiquid investment. Granted there are times when it is easy to sell real estate. Today however that is not the case.

Most people get into trouble by believing all that garbage on television about easy money in foreclosures. Listen to me here, because this is very important. There is a very valid reason why that house went into foreclosure. In most cases, what happened was that somebody sold someone a home that was way over inflated in value. In addition, the neighborhood that that house resides in is more than likely a depressed area for property values. If you buy that house for $300, that is not going to change the fact that this house is still in a depressed area. In addition, what you will find is that criminals will destroy the property every time you go in and spend money on it. They will splatter graffiti on the walls, they will destroy the sheet rock, and they will steal the air conditioner and anything else they can get their hands on. You will be thrown into a vicious cycle of spending money trying to make the property saleable or rentable, but you will be fighting a losing battle. You cannot win this battle. Your credit will be at risk, because of it. Buying foreclosures, in my opinion is a stupid thing to do, unless you buy a beach house in an area worth a lot of money. You are not going to be able to buy a beach house for $300.00. You will get the kind of property that I just described instead.

Perhaps you have watched those shows on television about people flipping houses for an easy profit. Yes, you may be able to find a lender who will loan you the money, but that does not mean that you should make these decisions without a lot of thought. If you make a bad purchase on a house that you thought you could flip, then you will find that you have another mortgage to pay. Who knows how long you will have to pay it? It could be years if your timing is wrong, or your fixer upper needs much more fixing than you anticipated. You have to be smart about your real estate decisions. Keep the emotions out of it. Use a real estate professional who is on your side and truly looks out for you.

The EquityKey Real Estate Option is a unique solution for senior clients who need money but who do not want to incur debt in the process. EquityKey LLC is a real estate investment company based in California. Certified Financial Planners started it in 2004. Their idea was great, their business model was great, but they only had one source of funds, which created a problem, which I will get to a little later.

They offered a Real Estate Option Program, which is quite simply a shared appreciation agreement between the owners of residential, investment, commercial, or vacant land properties and EquityKey LLC or one of their affiliates. This program was only available in states that have advantageous real estate, such as California, New York, Florida, Massachusetts, Arizona and other states that are appealing to seniors aged 65 through 85.

EquityKey would pay the owner of the property somewhere between 10 and 15% of the appraised value of the property for the right to share in the future appreciation of it. This appreciation percentage is 50% of the future appreciation.

If a husband and wife both participate in the EquityKey program, then they can sell 100% of the future appreciation in a Real Estate Option to EquityKey. In return, they will receive 20 to 30% of the appraised value of the property.

As you know, home equity does not earn any return. It is true that real estate appreciates, depending on the location of course. However, home equity earns a zero rate of return. Although lately, real estate has been going straight down as you know.

Seniors typically learned long ago to pay off their property as fast as they could. Most of them have done this. Unfortunately, they find themselves real estate rich and current income poor. This is even more true today after this recession of 2008 and 2009.

The EquityKey Real Estate Option filled a void since it allowed seniors age 65 to 85 that can qualify to obtain equity out of their property without a loan. No debt, no credit check, no interest payment, no closing costs upon signing and it is not a reverse mortgage. There is only a small $300 application fee that is refunded if you do not qualify. In addition, it is refunded if your payment is funded. You would only lose the $300 if you paid the fee, qualified and then backed out. The $300 goes towards the appraisal costs and let us EquityKey know that you are interested in going ahead.

Reverse Mortgages have their place in certain circumstances, but you have to pay back your equity at death. The bank received all of the interest on your home while you were paying for it. They did not pay you anything when you paid extra principal. They made you qualify to get a home equity line of credit and now they are taking your own money back in the form of a Reverse Mortgage! The EquityKey Real Estate Option is another alternative for those that can qualify.

Qualify? What I mean by qualifying is that EquityKey will collateralize their payment to you with a life insurance policy. If you are a smoker or in bad health, then you cannot qualify for the EquityKey Real Estate Option program. You have to be insurable, or reasonably healthy.

If you understand stock options, then you can probably understand the EquityKey Real Estate Option. Assume that you wanted to sell a covered call on IBM stock for example with an exercise price of $110 and it was currently trading at $100. By selling the option on IBM, you would receive the premium income for the option. If the price of IBM stays below $110, then you get to keep the premium income. If the price of IBM goes above $110, then the Buyer of the Call on the other side of your transaction can exercise the call option, take your IBM stock, and pocket the gain over and above $110.

With the EquityKey Real Estate Option, EquityKey is the Buyer of the Option and you as the property owner are the Seller of the Option. EquityKey is paying you a premium that is yours to keep. If EquityKey does not exercise their option on your property, then they simply walk away. You do not have to pay them back. EquityKey gets their money back by owning the life insurance policy.

The current equity that you have in the property at the time of the execution of the EquityKey Real Estate Option Agreement is yours to keep. You are only sharing in the *future* appreciation of the property. The 50% number scares some seniors because it seems like a large amount, but it is really a smaller number. For example, if a house is worth $500,000 today and ten years later it is worth $700,000, then EquityKey would receive $100,000 ($700,000 - $500,000 = $200,000 / 2 = $100,000.) One hundred thousand divided by $700,000 is 14.29%. This is the true percentage that EquityKey gets in this example. The return for EquityKey in this example is 4.81% assuming they gave you $62,500 as an EquityKey Option Fee up front. My trusty HP-12C calculator told me so.

EquityKey requires a life insurance policy on the property owner that they pay for and are 100% beneficiary of regardless of whether the homeowner sells their house down the road or not. This life insurance protects EquityKey in the event that the homeowner dies early and or the home fails to appreciate at all, or declines in value.

The minimum amount of appraised property value for residential or investment property is $350,000. It is $2,000,000 for commercial property and $3,000,000 for vacant land.

You must have 20 to 30% equity in the residential property. You can have an existing mortgage on the property and or an existing home equity line of credit. In addition, you can still refinance or get a new home equity line of credit subject to the same 20 to 30% limitations.

There are many advanced planning ideas available with the EquityKey Real Estate Option. Sophisticated clients see the advantages to enhance current income, enhance their investment portfolio, fund their grandchildren's college education, upgrade their properties, protect against Long Term Care expenses, replace loss income with more death benefit, contribute to a favorite charity, reduce debt, buy more property, travel or help family members.

My favorite use of the EquityKey Option Payment is for paying the taxes on an IRA to Roth conversion. If you had $300,000 in an IRA account, would you convert it to a Roth IRA all at once? You would probably not do this, because of the taxes that you would have to pay. Let us suppose that you took the EquityKey Option Payment and paid the taxes. This would allow you to convert your IRA to a Roth without affecting your current income or current investments. Remember, since it is considered an option for tax purposes, it is not taxed until it is exercised, sold or lapses. Therefore, in effect you are using this to your advantage.

There is no other place that I know of sans an interest free family loan where you can get access to funds to pay the taxes. Even if you did the Roth conversion and later wanted out of the EquityKey Real Estate Option Agreement, you could pull money out of the Roth tax free to solve that situation. If you stick with the agreement however, you do not have to ever pay it back.

I like using the EquityKey Option Payment for Roth conversions, solving Long Term Care needs, College Funding and Charitable donations myself. I think those four are the best uses of the funds.

EquityKey had some competitors who went bankrupt after a short time. Even EquityKey has run into some troubles with funding sources drying up. Their idea for the EquityKey Real Estate Option was good, but having only one funding source is bad. They should have never allowed themselves to depend on only one funding source. That was not smart. Who knows if they will be able to continue as an ongoing business? I hope that they are successful in finding more funding, because they have a good concept. What typically happens in times like these is somebody else steps up to the plate and provides the funding. It has to be a profitable venture for both the seniors and EquityKey. I wish them the best. They say that they will be back in the saddle here sometime around March of 2009. Only time will tell.

INSTALLMENT SALE TRUST

There are of course normal real estate transactions that we can assist you with. In addition, we now know that the capital gains tax rate will go back to 20% in 2011. We have a way of deferring capital gains taxes via an Installment Sale Trust whether the rate is 15%, 20% or more. A typical installment sale is where the owner of property agrees to sell their property to a buyer who wants to make payments. When the seller receives those payments, some of it is considered a return of principal, another part is subject to ordinary income taxes because it is interest income and the last part is the portion subject to capital gains taxes.

The main problem with installment sales is some buyers will default on the payments to the seller. Another problem is that the seller wants all the proceeds at once which means they have to pay all the taxes at once. If however, they chose to setup an Installment Sale Trust with a corporate trustee, then it may be the best of both worlds. The buyer would have to be fully capable of paying the full asking price. The proceeds would be paid into the Installment Sale Trust where the corporate trustee would pay them out according to the terms of the installment sale agreement. It is that simple.

The best part about this approach is that the capital gains taxes are frozen. In other words, if you elect a 20-year term for the payback, then 1/20 of the capital gains taxes are paid each year. The other 19/20's are reinvested to produce additional income for the trust beneficiaries. If the capital gains go up in the future, then you would owe the higher rate, but since you set up the Installment Sale Trust, you are only paying 1/20th per year.

Installment sales are only for property or businesses not stocks. In other words, you cannot do an installment sale on low cost basis stock. You used to could do Private Annuities with low cost basis stock, but the IRS nipped that strategy in the bud.

If you are interested in setting up an Installment Sale Trust, then you probably want to speak with me about it. There are not a lot of financial advisors who know about this strategy.

INVESTMENT PLANNING

We like the indexing approach and now we have the best investment vehicle for building your portfolio. It is not mutual funds, but rather Exchange Traded Funds.

Exchange Traded Funds are very low cost investments that trade like a stock. Pay attention here because this is very important to understand. If you invest in a mutual fund, you are invested with everyone else who owns shares of that fund. Regardless of when or how you invested in that fund, you are subject to the whims of the other investors in that fund. You have to pay taxes on the fund each year based on the ins and outs of the other investor's behavior. In essence, you have no control over the tax implications.

This is not the same with Exchange Traded Funds. When you buy shares of an Exchange Traded Fund, you have your own cost basis. It does not matter what other investors who own the same Exchange Traded Fund do. You only pay taxes when you sell it and when the fund pays it usual and customary income. There are no sudden unexpected large capital gains as there are with mutual funds. Although, we will certainly look at how 2008 ends up with regard to distributions. So far, so good from what I have seen.

The Exchange Traded Funds that we recommend are pretty much plain vanilla index funds with very low turnover costs. In addition, the expenses on these Exchange Traded Funds or ETF's when placed in a portfolio tend to be 0.35% or less. Mutual fund average expenses tend to be 1.07% or more according to the Investment Company Institute Fact book for 2008.

In addition, the turnover costs in mutual funds rob investor's savings everyday. For example, if a large mutual fund manager wants to sell a large position of a stock, this will typically make the price of that stock go down. The reason for this is that they are selling a large quantity of it in a short period of time. Then, when they have to reinvest the proceeds of their sell, they start buying a large position in another stock. This typically causes the price of the stock they are replacing to go up. The result is they buy fewer shares. The loss in value on the sell side and the loss on the replacement buy side are passed along to the mutual fund shareholder. There have been studies that say this is anywhere from one to 2% depending on the liquidity of the stocks in question. Add to that the normal fund expenses and you are looking at a hefty pile of expenses in fees and hidden fees to invest in mutual funds. Of course, do not forget about the tax implications either.

Mutual funds also do bad in bear markets. When investors are panicky and want to sell, then the mutual fund has to sell everything. This means that they may be forced to sell their profitable positions because there is such a strong sell demand. If they are forced to sell, then this spins off taxes. This is bad for you by the way.

ETF's on the other hand, buy a portfolio of stocks based on an index of stocks like the S&P 500 or Russell 2000. If a big institution buys ETF's and they want to sell, the ETF firm hands them back the individual stocks. Then, the institution has to sell the stocks, not the ETF firm. Therefore, the investor is saved from this turnover loss. In addition, the expense ratios on some ETF's are as low as 0.09%. As an investor, you save on both turnover costs and expense ratios, and you have your own tax basis in the positions. Nothing could be finer.

BEING AGGRESSIVE IS NOT A
FINANCIAL ROADMAP FOR SUCCESS

Most of us cannot handle the downside risk of a bear market. We think we can, but we cannot. When you go down a slide, yes, you eventually hit the bottom, but you do not get back to the top unless you climb back up. It is not automatic. You certainly do not make it back to the top by being more *aggressive*.

I cannot tell you how many times I have heard statements like this from both customers and their advisors. "We are going to have to stay *aggressive* to get back to the top. This is the only way to make it back".

It just kills me when I hear this. For the sake of argument, let us assume you were one of the *aggressive* investors whose portfolio is only down the laughingly low figure of 50% since the market high. It took less than one year for it to drop 50%. During September, October and November of

2008, it went down before you could do anything about it. Somehow, you believe that if you stay *aggressive,* then you will make it all back before you know it. You are not being truthful with yourself.

If you had $200,000 before the bear market and you lost 50%, then you are left with $100,000. Fair enough? In order to get back to $200,000 you have to double your $100,000. This equates to a 100% return on your account. How long do you truly believe that it will take to make that 100% return? One year? Two years? You are dreaming if you believe this fantasy.

What if the bear market continues for just a scant six months more and you are still *aggressive* with your asset mix? That 50% loss will expand to 60 or 70%. Then, how many more years will you push out the possibility of achieving your life goals? If you consider the old rule of 72's, then you know that your investment will double every 6 years if you earn 12% on average each year. This is of course assuming that the markets are tame for the next six years and another bear market will not happen while you are trying to recoup your $100,000. People, this is just to get back to even! Just look at the year 2008 if you do not believe it can happen.

If you are thinking about staying *aggressive* in order to recoup your losses, then you had better reconsider. You are setting yourself up for failure.

What if on the other hand, instead of being aggressive, you decided to be a little more moderate to conservative with your investment portfolio? Then, assume again that the bear market continued for another six months. Instead of going down another 20% by staying *aggressive,* you only went down another 6%. How much better off would you be? I would venture to say you would probably be a year or more ahead of the *aggressive* position.

This is not rocket science here. If you minimize your losses, then you will be better off. You do not have to achieve a higher return, because you did not take a big loss. Therefore, the catching up you have to do with a more moderate to conservative portfolio is a whole lot less.

Everyone is chasing performance. We all want to be the one who makes 50% in one year. Our fixation on performance has blinded us to the fact that we must choose only the best performing investments. Investors routinely ignore these prophetic words:

Past performance is not indicative of future performance.

How many times have we all read this? Better yet, how many times have we ignored it? I would guess way too many times. Now, our thinking is so messed up that we do not just want to make 50% in one year, we want to and expect to make 100% in one year. This is pure insanity and very ridiculous.

Sometimes you have to go to cash, too. That is what we did on October 6, 2008. Why did we do that instead of sticking with the supposedly tried and true diversified asset allocation approach? I saw some contradictions in asset class movements that were not supposed to diverge in such an extreme manner. Once I saw that, I was out. There was something "rotten in Denmark".

I saw a financial advisor on Fox Business that they were touting as the person who got out of the market on October 8, 2008. I beat him by two days. Maybe I should be on Fox Business, what do you think?

ALTERNATIVE INVESTMENTS ARE COMPLICATED

An alternative for people who have all their eggs in one basket is to buy into an Exchange fund. Typically, this strategy is for those with $1,000,000 or more in one stock and who have a 10 to 12 year time horizon. Do not confuse an Exchange fund with Exchange Traded Funds (ETF's), because they are not the same.

An Exchange fund is managed professionally. The portfolio is made up of investors who hold large positions in one stock. They all contribute their (different) stock to the Exchange fund. There may be 60 investors who contribute roughly a million dollars or more a piece. Now, their concentrated position is perhaps 1/60th of the Exchange fund. The manager of the Exchange fund sells a little each year, thus spreading out the capital gains taxes over time. You have solved a couple of problems. You have traded your concentrated position for a diversified portfolio of companies that is professionally managed and you have reduced your risk. Further, you have a better opportunity to handle the capital gains taxes. Moreover, if you change your mind, you can get your concentrated position back less fees and expenses.

The drawback to an Exchange fund is that they typically have upfront commissions and ongoing management fees. In addition, you generally have to commit to a long period of 10 to 12 years before you can begin to make regular withdrawals. Who is disciplined enough to do that?

Another type of investment that has proven very popular in recent years is a Hedge fund. There are several types, some of which are complex and others simple to understand. I like to keep things simple myself. In that simplistic vain of thinking, hedge funds take opposite positions on the market and typically try to neutralize their portfolios against major losses. They typically charge as much as 20% of the return on the account. In other words, if they make 20%, then the manager gets 20% of the 20% return or 4% for a management fee. If they do not make a profit, then ordinarily they do not take a management fee, or perhaps just a small one, like 3% of your accounts. They all differ in some respect, however.

Perhaps the biggest misconception about Hedge funds is that people think they return a lot of money. Their primary purpose is to conserve capital and take advantage of inefficiencies when they can. A true hedge would be 50% long the market and 50% short the market. Well, it would not make a whole lot of sense to have this kind of portfolio, since your return would be less than zero when you factor in commissions and fees. Come to think of it. A zero percent return does not sound all that bad today.

Hedge funds utilize futures, options, and leverage to make bets one way or the other on the market direction. When they are right, they do well. When they are wrong, they lose money. You typically need a larger amount of money to invest in one of these and you must meet the definition of an accredited investor with a million plus in net worth.

Of course, the New York person scandal will make everyone re-think putting money with a Hedge fund. If a person has his own broker/dealer and produces his own account statements, instead of Schwab, Fidelity, Pershing or TD Ameritrade producing them, then you had better watch out. If he controls the printing press, then there is the rub. Throw in a big ego, power and fame and there you have it. That is a scandal waiting to happen. This was a sad, sad lack of moral values and no real belief in God and doing the right thing, in my humble opinion.

Hedge funds are not for everyone. If you are dead set on finding a Hedge fund and you have limited funds, there are ways to create your own Hedge fund. You can buy Market Neutral mutual funds, or split your funds between a Short Index fund and a Long Index fund. If you go the latter route, then you had better be wary. Your chances of success go way down when you play this game by yourself. If you guess wrong, then you lose.

The important thing that I want you to remember is that you can do something to solve some of these more complex issues. The only problem you are likely to encounter is finding someone who knows what is an Exchange fund or a Hedge fund.

MISTAKES

I would like to offer my apologies to the fictional character Gordon Gecko from the movie, *Wall Street*. Greed is not good.

Bear markets have a tendency to humble us. We are floating along thinking we are making great decisions with our investments. Then the bear comes out to eat.

We keep telling ourselves that these are good companies and they will come back. In the meantime, we wait and watch our assets go down and down and down. In addition, if we were crazy enough to be on margin, our portfolio goes down twice as fast. Margin calls abound. Now we have to sell something, because we have no funds to add to the account. What do we sell? We can only deduct so much from our taxes. There comes a point where another capital loss means nothing to us. We surely do not have many capital gains left to offset, or we do not want to take them now. Is this anyway to run a portfolio? Do not let the market control you.

If you are going to buy stocks on margin, then you had better be prepared to "pay the piper". Margin means loan. You are borrowing against your assets. The best use of margin is for short-term cash flow needs where you know that other funds will be available that you can add to the account in a few weeks. If you stay on margin all the time, then brokerage companies will love you until they call you for more money and you cannot pony up. Be careful with margin loans. They can ruin you if you are not careful.

Sector Investing is a Mistake, too

There is another area where I see many talented people making huge mistakes. Some financial professionals recommend you invest in companies that you know. This means for example, that if you are in the telecommunications industry, then invest in mainly telecommunications companies. They kid themselves into believing that they know what they are doing. They diversify by buying wireless companies, handset manufacturers, and the baby bells.

What is wrong with this picture? When a telecommunications analyst comes out with his downgrade of any one of those stocks, the whole portfolio begins to crumble. This is really sector investing. Sector investing is subject to (yes, it is hard to believe but) the business cycle. That means sectors fall in and out of favor. This is nothing new. This has been going on a very long time. Only people have been blind to the fact.

The Mistake that Most People Make

Another way to invest is by concentrating your investments in one main stock. I think it was Andrew Carnegie who said, "Put all your eggs in one basket and watch that basket". There are tons of people out there who believe very strongly in their company. As a result, they concentrate their wealth in their own company stock. Many a millionaires have been born this way.

Ask the people who built up a large position in Lucent how they feel today. What about the people who worked for companies like Bear Stearns, Citi Group, Lehman Brothers, Washington Mutual, Countrywide Financial, Bank of America or even the once mighty Merrill Lynch. I bet they would tell you it was a dumb idea to put it all in their company stock. They know they should have diversified, especially, if they were close to retiring. It is even worse if they were laid off and now their 401(k) has dropped 50% or more when they may have to tap into that account to survive.

If you have more than 30% of your portfolio in one stock, you tend to lose the effect of diversification. You end up living and dying by what that one stock does. Again, it does not take a smart fellow to figure that out.

No Statistics Please

It is not my intention to bore you with a bunch of statistics and charts. Think about this. I am sure someone along the way has shown you a Mountain Chart of the stock market beginning in the 1920's. The result is small cap stocks outperformed, large cap stocks, international stocks, T-Bills, inflation and cash over the last seventy plus years. What does this have to do with you? Not a blooming thing.

I say this, because I have seen so many of you in my career put so much emphasis on security performance, especially when it comes to picking mutual funds. You will read magazines out the kazoo. You will do screens on the Internet. You will spend countless hours agonizing over which fund is the best. When you finally decide on which fund to invest in, then you throw your money at it and invariably watch it immediately lose value. At this point, you will agonize some more on whether you should sell it. Typically, you will begin to question whether it was a good fund or not. Moreover, usually within a very short time period, you will finally sell it at a loss and start the vicious cycle all over again.

Investing in a rear view mirror does not work. If you did a screen on mutual funds for the best performing funds over the last 75 years, what do you think you will find? Small cap stock funds (or, Aggressive Growth) are the clear winners.

I could have saved you a whole lot of trouble. All you have to do is look at that Mountain Chart again and realize that small cap stocks are the best place to be. Does this mean that you should put all your money in small cap stocks? No.

Conversely, you could do another mutual fund screen for Aggressive Growth funds for the last 15 years and you will find that they are one of the worst performing categories. Yes, I mean to tell you that if you just starting being *aggressive* 15 years ago, you would have been better off in an S&P 500™ index fund. How prophetic is that statement?

I have met only one person who has ever held onto the same mutual fund for a long-term time horizon. She has held onto this one mutual fund for over 50 years. She is still holding on to it as of the last time I spoke with her. The beneficiary of her life will be the one to sell it. What a testament to discipline and self-sacrifice she is! Could you hold onto to your mutual fund for 15 years? What about 10 years? Perhaps 5 years? Unfortunately, the average holding period for equity mutual funds is less than 3 years. Three lousy years is ridiculous, isn't it?

Think about that for a minute. I would speculate that 90% or more of you holding onto the same investment for 15 years or more is slim.

When you design a portfolio of investments, the fact is that over time the mix of investments that you choose will revert to a mean return for that period. If you have primarily blue chip stocks in your portfolio, then your volatility (vicissitudes) will be similar to the overall market. Go back and look at the yearly returns of the S&P 500™ index. Then, you will see what the volatility of such a portfolio will do.

Now think for a moment how a portfolio of 60% blue chip and 40% aggressive growth would react. Obviously, sixty percent of it would act like the market and the other portion would move like the aggressive growth category. It would just be a math calculation to see what additional risk you would be taking.

Let us examine this further. Assume that a portfolio is made up of 90% aggressive growth stocks and 10% cash. The volatility of this portfolio would have a much wider range of fluctuation.

Further thinking would help us to realize that if we increased the cash, or fixed income component of our portfolio, then we would reduce our volatility and along with it the risk of our portfolio.

What most people do not realize is that every portfolio has an expected return over a risk free rate of return. Depending on the amount of risk that portfolio is taking determines the return. There comes a point where you can significantly increase the risk of a portfolio, but not have the same increase in the return of the portfolio. This means that it does not make sense to take on 50% more risk for only a 2% chance of a better return. If there is no reward for the additional risk, then why take it on?

Most people think that they should invest in blue chip companies primarily. Therefore, they design (and I use that term very loosely) their portfolio with big blue chip issues. Their portfolio ends up having a return similar to the overall stock market.

Typical large company stocks like General Electric, Wal-Mart, Coca-Cola and so on are constantly in the news. They are releasing information everyday sometimes numerous times a day. Is there any big secret here? I do not think so. If you think that having a portfolio of blue chip companies is going to do anything but perform like the overall market, then you are wrong.

Have you ever seen a large company stock jump up 20% in one day? It may have happened on a rare occasion in the last seventy years, but it is certainly not typical. There will be difficulties and the overall return of a primarily blue chip portfolio will have an average return of the market. That is a fact Jack.

Small cap stocks are generally younger companies that have a niche idea, service, or product. There is usually no analyst following them in the beginning. Therefore, when they come out with that great product or service they have significant obstacles to their success. One of those obstacles is obtaining financing. Therefore, the small company management team promotes their idea to venture capitalists (VC's) who give them start up money. Usually, the VC's give them a few rounds of financing in exchange for stock. Then, when the company goes public and the lockup period has expired, the VC's sell their stock (hopefully for a handsome profit.) These people get all the IPO's.

Think for a moment if you are a mutual fund manager. Your job is to find good companies to invest in to improve the performance of your portfolio for you investors. The way you do this is by visiting these small companies. You find out about their great product before anyone else. Therefore, you buy the stock. You hold it until the company becomes popular in the marketplace. The small company begins to be noticed in the marketplace and the stock starts to creep up. Then, the small company signs a big distribution contract and the next thing you know, the stock shoots up. As a mutual fund manager, if you pick the right company, then you are well rewarded. If you do not pick the right company, then you will lose.

Small companies will *at times* tend to outperform large companies. So, does this mean load up on small companies? No, it most certainly does not. It just means that you should have some exposure to small companies in your portfolio. Without a doubt, it does not make sense to have portfolio of aggressive growth, or only small companies. Not all small companies make it. You have heard of bankruptcy, haven't you? Lately, there has been more talk of the burn rate. When the smaller companies burn through their cash and the venture capital funds dry up, then down goes the stock.

In 2008 and 2009, do you think small companies may have a little trouble raising funds? I would think so.

Large companies have a place in your portfolio as well as midcap companies. Of course, some international equity exposure may also be appropriate in a portfolio. Fixed income, real estate, commodities and cash are also crucial to designing a portfolio.

PARALYZED BY FEAR, ARE WE?

You have gone from one extreme to another. A few short years ago, you were loaded up with growth stocks, technology stocks, and *aggressive* growth mutual funds. Today, you are sitting on a pile of cash and a 2% CD looks appealing to you. What happened?

You violated the rules. Rules? What rules? The rules of portfolio design. Oh, you mean I have to actually put together a plan of portfolio design for my assets. There in lies your problem.

Most people go through life working and accumulate their wealth along the way. Periodically, when they get a wad of cash from a bonus, improved cash flow, or an inheritance, they "look for a place to put it". I got you on that point, didn't I?

If an investor was to go talk to an insurance person, then they are liable to come out with a life insurance policy and a variable annuity. If they go see a bank representative, they are liable to own a CD, some loaded mutual funds, or a little of both. If they seek out help from a wire house representative (full service brokerage firm,) then they might be sold some hot stocks, auction rate preferred's, CDO's or the flavor of the month mutual fund family. In addition, if they choose to go with an online broker and do it themselves, then they will end up buying something that has great past performance, but has little or no relevance to the current economic conditions.

All of the above choices make us accumulators. We accumulate various investments over time. We make decisions based on the moment that the cash is in our hands. Look at yourself today. You are probably making decisions, or have already made decisions to move a larger portion of your portfolio into safe investments. You are paralyzed by fear, so you make the safest and least painful decision. You are probably thinking, "I am already down 50%. I don't want to lose the other 50%". Why did you wait until you were down 50% is my question? It proves my point that you did not have your portfolio invested properly. You really need to get this point people. If it was not invested properly when it was 50% higher, it is not invested properly when it is 50% lower! Do you get that?

You have thrown the baby out with the bath water. You are still making decisions based on what you think is the best one to make today, given the losses that you have incurred previously. The decisions that you are making are based on fear. What you and most everyone else are missing here is a critical point.

Why did my portfolio decline so badly? You violated the rules of portfolio design. You over-allocated your dollars just as you are doing today with CD's, cash and cash equivalents. Except back then, you were putting the bulk of your assets into *aggressive* growth.

The Trend is not your Friend

Sometimes it is hard for people to get this point. If you are investing *aggressively*, then you expect the trend to continue. If you are investing conservatively, in CD's and money markets, then you expect the trend to continue.

Did I say that you expect the trend to continue? When you expect the trend to continue, then you are placing a bet at the crap table. Can you win at craps? Occasionally you can. Can you win at being aggressive? Occasionally you can. The reverse is also true. Occasionally you can win by being in CD's and money markets just as we did by going to cash on October 6, 2008. However, the critical underlying mistake here is that your investment choices are based on the trend to continue. You expect it to be good times all the time if you invest aggressively. Conversely, you expect it to be bad times all the time if you invest in CD's and money markets. By the time you read this book, I will probably be back in the market invested according to my strategy. I could care less if I miss the exact bottom. I do not try to make the best return out there. My approach is to conserve capital in down markets. This is what we do.

What would have happened if you had invested your money to take advantage of both good *and* bad years?

That is a novel idea. I should design my portfolio for both good *and* bad years. That way I can take advantage of a strong economy and I can take advantage of a weak economy. Wait just a darn minute. How I am supposed to do that? You design your portfolio so that you are never over-weighted.

Your portfolio could have been properly designed on Jan 1, 2000 and at the end of December in 2002, you could have had made money on your account. This is instead of losing on average over 14.8% or so for each of those years. Did you lose more than 14.8% per year in each of those three years? If so, then you were too, dare I say it, *aggressive.*

Even recently, from October 9, 2007, which was the recent peak of the market in 2007 until November 20 2008, the S&P 500 Index lost about 46% by my HP 12C calculations. A lot of you probably lost more than that because you were repeating the mistakes of 2000, 2001 and 2002. You did it again. You invested close to 100% in the stock market.

Listen to me folks. Never and I mean never ever, invest anything near 100% in the stock market. It is a huge mistake to do so. Go back in history and look at your patterns of investing. I guarantee you that you violated my two rules. One is you had more than 20% in one asset class and the other is that you put more than 65% in the stock market. Tell me that this is not true. You cannot. Every single time you have lost money investing this has been the case. Too much invested in one asset class and too much invested in the stock market. When you put both together, you have nitro glycerin.

MODELS ARE FOR AIRPLANES

I have never seen so many Model Portfolios in all my life. Mutual fund companies have them. Insurance Companies have them. Full Service and Discount Brokerage companies have them. Banks have them. Third Party Administrators to pension plans and 401(k)'s have them, too.

Is a cookie cutter solution really, what you want? Whenever a financial services professional tries to paint you into a Model Portfolio, tell them that this is not what you want. Tell them to custom design a portfolio for you and your family. It should center around your values and what is important to you.

We have Model Portfolios of our own but we customize it to the investor based on existing positions, tax implications, and income needs. Our approach is more of a plan than a cookie cutter solution.

Here lies the problem. Model Portfolios are based on a snapshot of time, a mix of assets, and assumptions about how conservative or aggressive you are. Most of the time, the period being shown is one that benefits the presenting company. It generally does not match your time horizon and it is investing in a rear view mirror again.

Typically, the recommended mix of assets for a Model Portfolio is determined by the think tank of the presenting company. Most of the time, the mix of assets shown to you does not include all asset classes or investment styles. It only includes the ones that they sell or they "think" are best for you. Do you think a mutual fund company is going to include an asset class of Real Estate Investment Trusts (REIT's) in their Model Portfolios if they do not have a Real Estate Investment Trust mutual fund? I do not think so. It makes you wonder, what else are they leaving out?

Most Model Portfolios are abysmal because they are typically too aggressive. Usually you will see a Model Portfolio of 80, 90 or even 100% equities. This is failure waiting to happen. The next bear market will ruin this portfolio in a hurry.

Personally, I do not even like showing our Model Portfolios. The reason that I do not is because people then expect that kind of outcome. In order to really understand investing you must understand certain aspects of it. First, an investor investing in a portfolio on January 1 will have a different performance than an investor investing in the exact same portfolio on June 1 of a given year. As a result, the returns showing the performance history is meaningless for the future. Did I say it was meaningless? If I did not say it, then let me say it now. Past performance is meaningless.

INVESTMENT QUESTIONNAIRES

The obligatory Investor Questionnaire is one of my favorite examples for stupidity. All these financial service companies have them. Somehow, by just answering 10 simple questions, these companies know right where to classify you. If your score is low, then you are conservative. If you score higher, then you are aggressive. You as the client tend to go along with it, because after all, you answered the questions!

Most of these questionnaires have a question similar to this one. "How much of a decline would you be willing to accept in any given year in order to achieve your objectives?" Some of the questionnaires let you answer it. You just pick a number out of the air. There are others that give you suggestions like 0 to 5%, 5 to 10%, and 10% to 15% and so on. The truth is you do not really know the answer to this question, because you do not know how you will react in a bear market. All logic goes out the window in a bear market and most people sell at the most inopportune time, or even worse, they hold on to losers. Decisions are based on emotions rather than logic. The last thing on your mind is sticking to that "Investment Questionnaire". Come to think of it. You cannot even remember where that stuff is on your Model Portfolio any more, much less the answers to that questionnaire.

The biggest mistake in investing is not being able to accurately identify your risk level. More than anything else, you really need to address how much risk you can tolerate. Ask yourself this question. "What is the biggest drop that I have experienced as an investor in my portfolio in one year?" If it is less than 10% and you suddenly want to be 100% stocks, then boy are you in for a rude awakening.

Can you truly tolerate a 30 or 40% decline in the value of your account when you have less than 5 years to go until your desired retirement date? I do not think so. There is a better way folks.

The investment profession was told a few years ago to tell their customers about holding on through the bad times. The problem with this is that the asset allocation gets all out of whack. Some asset classes/styles go down more dramatically than others causing a deviation from your original objectives. You cannot just sit there and "hope" that the market comes back. You need to reposition and re-balance your holdings periodically. Other times, like this October of 2008, you have to go to cash because it is the smart thing to do. Another advantage of going to cash is that you can lock in tax losses for the year and possibly future years. After 31 days, you can reinvest at a lower cost basis and start again. You do not want to get back in before the 31 days is up. Otherwise, you are violating the wash sale rules of the IRS and they will disallow the losses.

If you lost more than 40% of your account balances here in 2008, then yes, I am talking to you. Do not just sit there and hope your account will come back. You need investment counseling and you need it now, especially because of what has happened. Look at it this way. You will get some new investment counseling at a 40% discount since your accounts are down 40%, so you are saving money!

The point that I wanted to make here is no more status quo Model Portfolios. If someone is trying to get you to invest your hard earned or inherited dollars with him or her, then make them work for it. You want an ongoing professional relationship that includes a plan and a process. An annual review should be the norm, whether or not you do it yourself, or hire a professional to help you.

Personally, I focus on protecting assets in a bear market. It is my claim to fame. There is no talk about how much of a return we are going to make you. Instead, we talk about how to invest in a defensive posture. The thinking is if you do not take a big decline, then you do not have to make as large a return. Reducing the volatility is the name of the game.

"It is easier to climb out of a shallow hole".

THE DREADED 10-YEAR TIME HORIZON

What is your time horizon? Investment professionals love it when you say 10 years or more. Why? Because they know they can get (dare I say it) *aggressive.*

"You have ten years or more until retirement, don't you? Well then, you can definitely be a little more *aggressive* with your portfolio". Have you ever heard this before?

Most inexperience professionals have this burning desire to put anybody with a time horizon over 10 years in a more *aggressive* portfolio. This just really blows my mind. Do they have a crystal ball? Do they know without a doubt that the next 10 years will be the best in history for being *aggressive?* The last 10 years did not prove this true. For that matter, do they even know whether you should be in stocks at all? Moreover, if so, what percentage in their professional opinion is the correct one for an *aggressive* portfolio?

Let me let you in on a little secret. They do not know. When an investment professional tells you that you can be *aggressive* with your portfolio, then tell them you are really a moderate type person. When you tell yourself you can handle an *aggressive* portfolio mix, look in the mirror and slap yourself in the face a couple of times. You need to wake up, because you are obviously asleep at the wheel.

The risk for being aggressive is not consistently worth it. The key word in that sentence is consistently. Do not get me wrong. People can have short-term success by being aggressive. However, they cannot do it consistently. I am teaching you about wealth accumulation here, not a get rich quick scenario.

A scant few years ago, you could have papered your wall with the *Wall Street Journal*, thrown darts at it, and made money. It is not so easy after the bear has come out to eat, is it?

What went wrong? There were simply too many *aggressive* and greedy investors. There was too much concentration of assets in startups and promising companies. The analysts poured gasoline on the fire when they made those outlandish growth assumptions. Sure, the Al Qaeda organization did not help matters, but the underlying economic problems were already in place long before September 11, 2001.

Are things different this time since September the 11th? I believe that they are. Your thought process has to be defensive oriented when it comes to your investments. God forbid Al Qaeda does anything during President Obama's first months in office, especially with the state of the economy the way it is. Do you think the market might go down in this scenario? Do not be foolish enough to believe that it cannot. It is always a possibility as long as these terrorists are around.

You should not focus on how much of a return you can make, but rather how can you protect your portfolio from losses. That has the makings of a smart investor.

The Internet Bubble

Here is an example of being caught up in the euphoria of the stock market heyday. Who can argue that DSL or fiber optics is not a great idea? If they are such great ideas, then why are you DSL Company declared bankruptcy? Do not get me wrong. Having DSL in the house would be great. Just raising my monthly cost from$14.95 per month to $49.95 per month and buying a new modem just does not seem worth it.

Imagine if you are running a small business office with six or seven computers tied to a network. The fiber optics idea (better known as the need for speed) crosses your mind as a great thing to do for your business. You call in the IT expert and he tells you that they are going to have to dig up the street and your driveway to bring the fiber optic cables into your building. Then, they are going to have to re-wire your whole building for fiber optics and pull out all the existing network lines that you have now. Then, those old routers and switches are going to have to go. You will not need them any more. What you need now is new routers and switches to handle this fiber optic cable. Oh by the way, do not forget those old Ethernet cards. You need to pull them out of all your workstations and of course replace them with the new cards. In addition, you may need to upgrade a workstation or two. After all is said and done, you are probably looking at $40,000 or $50,000.

I believe your first inclination is that fiber optics is not all that it is cracked up to be. The heck with this need for speed thing you tell yourself. "I see said the blind man". Now do you understand why new technology takes a while to become a standard?

If you are going to invest in one of these companies again, it had better be in small increments and for a very long time. In addition, perhaps most importantly, you had better be prepared to lose every dime you invest in this area. This is a "big dog gets the bone" business. That is a famous quip from my Dad, Hillman.

The Reality of Monte Carlo

A hot new topic in the financial planning community is Monte Carlo Simulation software. We first have to remember where we came from. In the past, we would take our trusty HP-12C calculator and figure out the future value of our current assets at an assumed interest rate. (I love my trusty HP-12C calculator.) This worked great for a long time. As a client, we would just pick a number that sounded good. "I want to earn 12% on my money". The financial professional loved to hear that, because again he or she could design an *aggressive* portfolio. Sound familiar?

Monte Carlo simulation software says that we cannot count on a steady 12% every year. There will be varying degrees of earnings each year. There will be negative growth years as well as positive growth years. The result of which will give us varying degrees of success in achieving our earnings goals. We have been painfully reminded about negative years here lately.

A Monte Carlo analysis runs through a ton of possibilities then provides us with a percentage chance of achieving our goal, like 72% for example. We know what 72% is. It is a C minus. We would rather have an A plus.

How accurate is a Monte Carlo simulation? In all probability, it provides a deeper understanding of the likelihood of achieving a specific financial goal. A hypothetical illustration of what may or may not happen is what it really is. Do you really need some software to tell you that the stock and bond markets go up and down? No, but knowing the difference in what will happen to your portfolio if the market goes down in the early years, or in the later years of accumulation may make you take a more realistic view of how to plan your future.

Think about it. If the market took a big drop in year one, but went on to do well in years two through five, then you would be doing a whole lot better than the reverse. That is, doing well in years one through four and then the big drop in year five as you are close to retiring. If you are planning your retirement, should you really assume the rosier scenario? Not unless you like setting yourself up for big disappointments.

Ponder this thought if you will. Monte Carlo simulation may help you realize that your portfolio could be like the early 2000's where the performance of the S&P 500 Index tanked. You may lose -14.84% for the first three years of your (dare I say it) *aggressive* portfolio. Jiminy Cricket! If your goal was 12% a year and the first three years you averaged a negative 14.84%, then you lost 80.52% of your objective! (12% minus a negative 14.84% = -26.84% x's 3 years = -80.52%) You have to make that up somehow, or you will never reach your goal. Maybe you need to be more *aggressive*. What ever you do, please do not do that.

How about another Monte Carlo possibility? Let us assume during your first 3 years you somehow managed to average 12%. Then, in year four, the bear comes out and you lose 25%. Let us make this simple. $100,000 invested compounded at 12% for 3 years. We have $112,000 at the end of year one. Year 2, we end the year with $134,400. Year 3, we have $161,280. Then in year four, we lose 25%. This leaves us with $120,960. In simple interest terms, after four years of being *aggressive*, this has netted you a whopping 4.87% annualized average return!

Invariably, you will focus on the fact that you had $161,280 at the end of year three and you lost around $40,000. You probably could have bought a guaranteed FDIC insured CD that would have done better than that. Oh well, you figure that your portfolio will "come back" with your *aggressive* mix of assets.

This is only a hundred thousand dollar example. Magnify that example out with a million dollars or more and you will see the huge impact that being too aggressive can have on your portfolio. Instead of only a $40,000 decline, with a million dollars to start with, then you are looking at a $400,000 decline. Ouch!

Monte Carlo simulation has taught you that these scenarios could happen to you. Therefore, you think about it for a split second longer, but get back to the fact that you are not being unreasonable by wanting a 12% return. After all, that Mountain Chart told you that historically it could be done. Therefore, you move your money to another brokerage firm, mutual fund family or other financial institution. Then, you go sit down with the new financial representative and he/she pulls out their Mountain Chart, gives you "their" Investment Questionnaire that determines that you are *aggressive*, places you in "their Model Portfolio" and then you repeat the same mistakes all over again.

You have to ask yourself, is the financial professional making the mistakes, or are you making the mistakes because your expectations are wrong. It is a tough call, but you really need to think about this. If your expectations are unreasonable and unachievable, then nobody can help you.

You really have to be fair and balanced with your expectations, or you will have failure after failure. Know thyself.

CHA-CHING

Is cost an issue in investing? Certainly it is. Let us take the alphabet soup of mutual funds first. There are A shares that typically deduct 5.75% from your funds on equity mutual funds and 4.75% on bond mutual funds. It does not take a smart person to figure out that your stock mutual fund starts out in the hole 5.75% and your bond fund 4.75% in the hole, simply stated. It is safe to say it is a bad idea to buy an A share bond fund, because it may take longer than a year to make 4.75% on a bond fund if interest rates are low. At least with the A share stock fund, you have a better opportunity to overcome the 5.75% if you are *aggressive*. Am I right?

The B Share is the mutual fund industry's answer to the no-load fund. They just build in more expenses to the fund so they can pay the financial professional their commission for recommending their fund. One hundred percent of your money goes to work immediately. It usually has a six-year penalty for early withdrawal. That is not a problem, because you have a ten-year time horizon. Remember?

C Shares are what the mutual fund industry dreamed up when they wanted to keep more of your assets on the books longer. They figure if they only charge you one percent (a year) *more* in expenses on top of the management fees, you would not mind because you can liquidate at any time without penalty after the first year. The financial professionals would like it, because they could build their book with C share funds with one mutual fund family and have a recurring income for the next several years. The mutual fund companies and insurance companies started printing glossy brochures showing financial professionals how they could build their own annuity with C Shares. The problem with C Shares is that it benefits everyone but you.

You may be asking, what are D shares, Y shares, or R shares. They differ from fund company to fund company. Some of these type shares have $1,000,000 minimums and others allow only financial advisors to purchase them. If you want to know, just ask a financial professional to find out for you. On the other hand, you could do something unique and read the prospectus!

No load funds are great investments if you just focus on the fact that they do not have A, B, or C type commissions. They do not have a commission at all. This is great!

No load funds like to tout the fact that they will save you money over the long haul with reduced expenses. Hey, how is that no load aggressive growth fund doing for you lately? Are you thinking about the expenses that you saved in buying it?

It is not what you pay. It is what you get in return. Yugos were cheap, don't you remember?

Expenses are only one of many items to think about when you are investing. However, expenses are not the only factor to consider. You have to know how to put it all together, or build your portfolio. It also matters how you manage the process as time goes on.

A new type of investment as I mentioned earlier has recently surfaced on the horizon. These new investments are called Exchange Traded Funds, or ETF's. They typically are an index fund based on some underlying asset class. They trade like a stock and therefore have a commission. The expenses on these investments are usually rather low. You can find an

S&P 500 Exchange-Traded Fund with an expense ratio of 0.09. Most mutual funds that invest in this index, charge anywhere from .10 to .50 in expenses. Therefore, you can save some expenses over mutual funds, but do not forget about the transaction costs.

You can design a great portfolio with ETF's especially if you are an individual investor. They are very popular with endowments, pension plans, and other institutions, also. You can buy Exchange Traded Funds that are value oriented, or growth oriented. The key thing to remember with ETF's is to minimize your transaction costs. What good is a low expense ratio if you drive up your transaction costs?

Lately there has been a barrage of new types of ETF's. Personally, I like to keep it plain vanilla. The couch potato socially responsible ETF fund just does not interest me like the plain vanilla ETF's do.

STOCK INVESTING

Investing in individual stocks is a completely different matter. There are expenses associated with buying a stock. In today's competitive marketplace, you can trade a stock for as little as $5. That is if you want to risk putting your money with a firm that is going to crash and burn any day now. Alternatively, you could pay up a little, to around $10 a trade and get with one of the major discount firms.

So, let us assume that we have $100,000 to invest. We split that $100,000 up into 20 stocks. We buy only market leaders. We diversify amongst different industries and sectors. We do our homework with regard to research. Our cost is 20 times $10 or $200. This is only 0.2% of our portfolio. That is a good expense ratio. What have we done? We have built our own index fund, except for the fact that we have to spend our time keeping up with twenty stocks. Now, we have to know when to sell. Oh by the way, how much are the expenses on an ETF Index fund? Generally, the expenses are about 0.1% or less.

I wonder. I guess I could have saved myself the headache of researching all those stocks and the sleepless nights I spent wondering whether to sell or not, by buying an ETF. Not to mention the fact that I would have cut my expenses a little bit on the front end. Sure, I might have ongoing ETF expenses, but 0.1% is worth it to not have to commit all of my time.

Nevertheless, you tell yourself that you like investing on your own. You think it is fun picking stocks. You believe that you can do better than some of the idiotic advice that you received in the past.

Yes. I would have to agree with that statement. There are some inexperienced people out there who just want to make money from you and are not concerned about helping you. But then again, there are highly professional people like me, too.

The problem with picking your own stock portfolio is holding yourself accountable. Are you going to fire yourself if you make some bad decisions on some stocks? Probably not, but you will surely hold an investment professional accountable wouldn't you?

Answer me this if you will. Did you ever think that you would see blue chip stocks trading at these prices? Bank of America at $4.70. General Electric at $11.26. So, tell me again, how confident you are in picking stocks. It is a loser's game to try to be a stock picker yourself. You may have some short-term success periodically, but eventually you will see a market like this one in 2008.

Investment professionals know that they are accountable and pay large sums, or their firms do to have sophisticated portfolio management tools for your benefit. Chances are that an individual do-it-yourself investor does not pay $15,000 a year for research and a portfolio management program. They use the free Internet sites to keep up with their portfolios. Most investors think they know what their returns are, but I have met a scant few that really do. Again, you get what you pay for. Cheaper is not always better.

SOLUTIONS: MAJOR LESSON FOR INVESTORS

If you are an investor, do not ask to see an investment adviser's performance. You probably think that I am crazy for saying this, but believe me I am not. Let us assume that I am your investment adviser, I show you my performance for the last 10 years, and it averages 8.14%. (I just picked a number out of the air here.) Therefore, as the investor, in your mind, you immediately think to yourself that you will get 8.14% on your portfolio. This is the absolute worst way on earth you should decide to choose an investment adviser.

First, the last ten years may have been a period that favored that particular manager's style. For example, assume that the last ten years was a boom period for blue chip stocks and your investment adviser that you are considering is a blue chip stock manager. You make your decision to go with this investment adviser not realizing that the bull market for blue chip stocks is over. The next few years are awful for blue chip stocks and you cannot understand what just happened.

What you need to look at if you are evaluating an investment adviser has nothing to do with performance. You must look at their P-R-O-C-E-S-S. What is their process? What is their P-L-A-N? How do they make investment decisions? What asset classes are they investing in? What are the expenses? What are the tax implications of the asset mix? How much income can I expect from this portfolio plan? These are the questions to ask.

Forgot about performance! The performance will be there for you when you have a plan, a process, the right asset classes, low expenses, low turnover costs, a smart tax plan and a tax efficient income plan.

BACK TESTING THE 20%/65% RULE

The proof is in the pudding. Okay, I was pulling your leg about no statistics. The following hypothetical portfolio is a 45% equities, 55% fixed income and cash portfolio. By the way, hypothetical means make believe, or do not try this at home. In addition, 45% is below my maximum limit of 65% in equities. You can now do this with ETF's, instead of mutual funds. Below I am showing you the *index* returns.

This is not the actual ETF's. There would be minor differences because of tracking errors with the ETF's, but it is close enough for government work. In addition, you would have to factor in the fees being charged by the advisor and the transaction costs. In other words, if your advisor is charging a 1.50% annual fee, plus $19.95 per trade transaction costs, then those would have to be factored in. I am trying to push across a conceptual idea to you here.

This hypothetical portfolio is within the 20% style limitation and the 65% equities limitation mentioned in a previous chapter. If you will notice, there is nothing higher than 15% however. It is a little bit less aggressive with only a 45% equity position. For purposes of illustration only, (not for recommendation) I have chosen the following indexes:

$10,000	S&P 500 Citi:Barra Value	10%
$5,000	Russell Mid Cap Value	5%
$10,000	Russell 2000 Value	10%
$5,000	MSCI EAFE	5%
$5,000	MSCI Emerging Markets	5%
$10,000	Cohen & Steers Realty Majors	10%
$15,000	Barclays Capital 1-3 Year U.S. Credit	15%
$10,000	Barclays Capital Intermediate U.S. Govt./Credit	10%
$15,000	Barclays Capital U.S. Govt./Credit	15%
$10,000	Barclays Capital US Treasury TIPs	10%
$5,000	Schwab Value Advantage	5%
$100,000		100%

The hypothetical index portfolio is compared against market indexes below. These are the *cumulative* index returns for the various time periods through January 31, 2009. These are not annualized returns. This is the *cumulative* point A to point B return for each time period.

	One Year Cumulative Return	3 Yr Cumulative Return	5 Yr Cumulative Return	10 Yr Cumulative Return
Index Portfolio	-19.84%	-9.31%	6.72%	+57.95%
S&P 500	-38.63%	-31.34%	-19.50%	-23.53%
Russell 3000	-38.86%	-32.39%	-18.69%	-18.22%
DJ Total Market	-38.60%	-32.39%	-17.52%	18.96%
MSCI EAFE	-43.74%	-32.43%	-3.45%	-2.06%

These are the annualized returns for each time period:

	One Year Annual Return	3 Yr Annual Return	5 Yr Annual Return	10 Yr Annual Return
Index Portfolio	-19.84%	-3.21%	1.31%%	4.68%
S&P 500	-38.63%	-11.78%-	4.24%	-2.65%
Russell 3000	-38.86%	-12.23%	-4.05%	-1.99%
DJ Total Market	-38.60%	-11.87%	-3.78%	-2.08%
MSCI EAFE	-43.74%	-12.255	-0.70%	-0.21%

Take a look at the *Index Portfolio* performance on an annual basis. From January 31, 2008 through January 31, 2009, it lost -19.84%. The other indexes, which are 100% stocks and against my 20%/65% Rule, lost over thirty-eight percent. Now you see that you can design a portfolio with only 45% in stocks and still beat the overall stock market both domestic and foreign. If you look at the 3 year, 5 year and 10-year annual returns, then you will see that it can also be done over a long-term period. The reason this is possible is because you have less volatility when you properly diversify your investments. Bear markets favor my strategy.

Now I want you to think about something for a minute. If you go see a financial advisor and they tell you that they made 10.41% for the last five years, then you want to do some research yourself. Go look up what the S&P 500 did for the same five-year period. In this case, the S&P 500 returned a negative -4.24%. A major red flag should go up immediately with this financial advisor. More questions should follow. How did the financial advisor do this? What assets classes did they invest in? If they tell you that it is a proprietary secret, then walk out the door. If they tell you that it was invested mostly in energy stocks, then go back and look at the last five years and see how energy stocks performed. This is easily done by looking at the performance of XLE, the Energy Select SPDR ETF. Then, assuming that the performance of that is close to 10.41%, then ask if they are a market timer, or sector rotation manager. This type of manager is inappropriate for most people. I would never want to put more than (guess how much) 20% in any once sector. Therefore, I would limit my investment to 20% and more than likely much less. Also, I would consider this as an asset class if they indeed were an energy sector manager. Is this making sense?

I am sure that you could have beaten the *Index Portfolio* above by tweaking it in some way. This is my obligatory disclaimer that there are other ways to have outperformed my hypothetical example. You could have used Short ETF's and Ultra Short ETF's, which are bear market funds that benefit when the market goes down. The problem with using those is you have to know when to get in and know when to get out. It is an educated guess done by professionals. I would not recommend playing this game.

Think about the S&P 500 from a dollar investment standpoint. A hypothetical 100% S&P 500 investment would have declined from an initial investment of $100,000 to $61,370 after one year. You do not have to be a smart person to figure out the fact that this is a stinging loss in asset value. You will look at your loss in terms of losing dollars ($38,630), not a percentage loss. That is assuming of course that you only risked $100,000, instead of say $500,000, or a million dollars. I shudder to think how much money would have been lost under those circumstances.

Let us see, which do I prefer? My initial investment of $100,000 to decline to $80,140, or my initial investment of $100,000 to decline to $61,370. You would have saved $19,000 in losses with my 20%/65% Rule. I know what you are thinking. I would not want to lose the $19,860 in the first place. I agree, but remember, this is assuming that your advisor did not get you out of the market. It is also assuming that you have no other safe investments like bonds, annuities or CD's.

We went to cash for our clients on October 6th, 2008. Most of the damage in the last year occurred after that date. My point here is even when you properly diversify, you still have to be adept at moving to cash sometimes. If your advisor did not go to cash, then you may want to rethink your advisor. Check that, you definitely want to rethink your financial advisor.

Do Not Fail To Understand This Point

How far will a mistake like this set you back from achieving your goals? You will need a 62.95% return to make it back to $100,000 in one year. That 62.95% return will be a moving target, too. My *Index Portfolio* will need 24.78% to make it back to $100,000. Did you get that? Look at that difference. There was only a 18.79% difference when it went down. However, there is more than double that when you try to recoup your assets.

This is critical that you understand the math with this example. By being aggressive, you lost 38.63%, but it will take a 62.95% return to make it back to $100,000. My Index Portfolio also lost money, 19.86%, however it will only need 24.78% to make it back to $100,000. My Index Portfolio has a *38.17% advantage* over the aggressive portfolio. This is 24.78% - 62.95% = -38.17% which is the percentage that you will need to overcome my Index Portfolio. This is only to catch up to it, not to mention outperform it.

Now, do you see why it is so critical to protect your downside risk?
You have to protect your downside at all costs. *Forget about the upside performance.* In order to be successful investing your money, you have to protect your downside risk. This is the secret to investing.

Let us take a harder look at this. Assume that you stay put and do not change a thing. Suppose that the market came back and you made 28.00% on your *aggressive* portfolio. My hypothetical portfolio only made 20.00%. Your aggressive portfolio outperformed me by 8%. Therefore, you think that you are going to make it back now. However, once again, you are assuming that your aggressive positioning is the best way to stay over time. Investors routinely make this fatal mistake over and over again. They assume that the current market trend will continue.

You may catch up to it someday, (I seriously doubt it, however) but the next bear market will knock you right back down again. The reason this is true is that you will be investing *assuming* it will always be a good time to be aggressive.

I will be a monkey's uncle. Will you look at this? The bear market came back in 2008. Why did you invest thinking this was not going to happen again? That is not smart.

I am sure some of you are still thinking that you are more experienced now because of what has happened in the recent bear market. Further, you probably believe that you will know when to jump out next time. This kind of thinking is not a financial strategy. It is a guessing game. The problem with this mentality is you have to be right from now on. One mistake will cost you big time. Do not play this game. You will lose.

Consider if you will, a $1,000,000 portfolio would be approximately $190,000 ahead of you, or a $2,000,000 portfolio would be almost $400,000 ahead of you, hypothetically speaking of course. Have I painted the picture for you? Let everyone else make mistakes with their money. Do not let this happen to you, ever again.

The above examples are buy and hold examples. I did not do the calculations assuming annual rebalancing. However, if you were to rebalance the portfolios to their original allocations each year, then you would probably improve your returns a little bit more. It is not going to be enough to get you excited however, because if you rebalance every year, then you have transaction costs every year. This tends to mitigate the rebalancing effort.

I could have run numbers for you until I turn blue in the face, but I think you are getting the picture by now. My strategy works and if you follow it, then you will be better off than following the herd. Never forget this:

It is easier to climb out of a shallow hole.

Remember, you make money by *protecting your downside.* Invest for good markets *and* bad markets, not one or the other. If sometimes you think you need to go to cash, then go to cash for crying out loud!

Build a financial strategy according to your personal values and your needs, goals and objectives. My wise counsel is to hire a competent professional, preferably one with few conflicts of interest. If you live in Florida or Indiana, then that means me.

Be Careful Out There

That reminds me of a situation that I ran into recently. Let me present this investment to you. Mr. and Mrs. Investor, I have this wonderful investment for you. It is a promissory note that pays you 12% interest. What we are doing is raising money for a Private Equity Placement. The money is going to be given to our general partners who are buying oil and gas royalties in Texas. There is a recently discovered oil reserve that their geologists say is going to pump out millions of barrels a day. They will use the money from your investment to buy the equipment that they need to get the oil out of the ground. Once the wells start pumping, then you will share in the oil revenues based on the amount you invested. It is a no lose situation.

How did that sound, especially like in early 2008 when the price of oil has sharply increased? Mark my word. You will see similar investment frauds such as this one where unscrupulous advisers will fleece many a dollars from unsuspecting investors. Do not be one of the ones that are caught up in this garbage.

Remember, P-L-A-I-N V-A-N-I-L-L-A with your investments. When people get into trouble, it is because they believe in something that will make them a whole lot of money. Look at the New York person scandal for proof. He *allegedly* appealed to greed by highlighting his so-called outstanding performance. Now we know the truth.

Reform Ideas

A Word about Regulations

Recently, I earned the Chartered Advisor for Senior Living designation by spending countless hours studying for it. Several regulators have all joined the cause that senior designations are evil and only a guise to bilk old people out of their money.

Anything that is a benefit to my clients seems to me to be a good thing. How can you be faulted for educating yourself? I just do not understand this thinking. Of course, I understand that there are bunches of bogus senior designations out there, but mine is not one of them. The CASL is 15 hours of college credit. I earned it from the American College in Bryn Mawr, Pennsylvania.

Of course, this New York person is not making my life any easier either. I am sure we will see more onerous rules and regulations because of his antics and the failures of FINRA to catch him.

An Oxymoron of Sorts

Let us look at both sides of the coin. If a stockbroker were to invest your money in a portfolio made up of either stocks or equity mutual funds, then what would be the expected downside possibility? Is this a number that you can quantify? Can you actually say that if you invest in this or that portfolio, then you can expect to lose potentially no more than "x" dollars? The answer to that question is of course unknown, because it depends on many different factors.

If we were to only think back to the bear market years of 2000, 2001 and 2002, then we would know what actually happened. The S&P 500™ index lost 9.1% in 2000, 11.89% in 2001 and 22.10% in 2002 according to

Wikipedia. Even consider the recent year of 2008 where the S&P 500™ dropped 37%.

In September of 2008, the Dow Jones Industrial Average had three brutal days. On September the 15th, 2008 the Dow Jones Industrial dropped 504.48, on the 17th the DJIA dropped 449.36 and on the 29th of September, it dropped 777.68 points in one day, all according to the relative facts on Wikipedia's Web site.

Let us not forget what happened in October and November of 2008, Ugly with a capital U. The stock market can go down and go down in a hurry. As an investor, you are taking the risk. This risk is for all practical purposes unknown.

For our clients, we got out of everything and went to cash on October 6, 2008. The only reason we got out in October instead of August of 2008 was that I changed firms. I was not officially licensed until October. It took about eight weeks for the transition of client accounts. When I became licensed, then we went to cash for all of our investment clients within a week of my being licensed at the new firm. Our portfolios were never fully invested, because we never put 100% in the stock market. Only fools do that. Yes, that is what I said. If you have 100% in the stock market, then you are a fool!

Of course, the question becomes, when do we get back in? First, I am not in the business of trying to pick a bottom. My objective is to protect our client's principal with growth as a secondary objective. Just as "I knew it when I saw it" in October 2008, I will know it when I see it to get back in. When I do get back in, again it will be with our standard reduced equity and asset class limits. Most likely in the 40 to 55% equity range.

We know one thing, if we had been 100% equity invested in the early 2000's or in 2008, then we would have lost lots of money. For some people, during the early 2000's it was 40% to 50% or more. In 2008, history repeated itself. The S&P 500 was off more than 40% from October 2007 to November of 2008 according to Wikipedia.

For the other side of the coin, let us assume that you bought a fixed annuity with a guarantee. Alas, I almost forgot they have surrender charges. Let us say that you bought one with a guaranteed rate of return. It could be a simple fixed rate of return set each year by the insurance company or it could be based on an index. There is a guarantee on the downside in that they protect your principal from loss. They may provide a minimal guarantee of say 1% or 0%, but in either case, there is no loss of principal.

Insurance agents are normally accused of two things. One is that if you are the insurance agent, then you are paid excessively high commissions for selling the annuity. The other thing is that they have excessively long surrender charges.

Personally, I do not understand why these issues have not been addressed long ago. Here is a little education about annuities. First of all, the Internal Revenue Service has a little something called the Internal Revenue Code that says there is a penalty for early withdrawal from an annuity if you are under age 59 ½. Is it no wonder then that most people who are attracted to annuities are over age 59 ½? These same fine folks are not very crazy about paying taxes. Therefore, they are the primary demographic for annuities. If the IRS were to lower the age to 40, then you would find that the primary demographic would be 40 and over for these products.

If you invest in the stock market, as I proved above, you have no idea really how much you can lose. If however, you invest in an annuity and you want to get out of it, then is it not true that you know exactly how much you would be penalized? Let us assume that you bought an annuity with a 10-year surrender charge and you need to surrender it in year 3. You know the surrender charge in year three is 7% of your original principal. Do you not know your downside loss potential is 7%? However, keep in mind that you get to keep the growth for those three years. The surrender charge is based on the original investment, not on the account value.

On the other hand, let us assume that you invested in the stock market and after three years, you need to get your money. However, the problem is that the stock market has trended down for three years. The odds are you have lost more than 7% in the stock market. When you cash out of the stock market, in this situation, you could be far worse off than if you cashed in an annuity. Never thought of it that way, did you?

Stockbrokers charge 5.75% for A share mutual funds and they can earn around 4.75% gross commissions on the sale. You lose that immediately from day one, by the way, while the stockbroker benefits financially. Nevertheless, if an insurance agent sells you an annuity that pays him or her 5%, then they are accused of putting their interests before the client. It does not matter that their product is guaranteed! The truth is they both put their own interests ahead of the client. Nevertheless, at least with annuities you know exactly what your potential loss may be.

Let me get this straight. My choice is to pay a stockbroker 5.75% where my investment is immediately worth 94.25% of my original investment and is not guaranteed. Alternatively, I can buy an annuity that is guaranteed and I can control how much my loss is each year. After I buy the mutual funds and lose 5.75% right away, it is then that the stock market decides to tank on me. The financial press advises against putting your money into annuities, but it is okay to put your money in mutual funds? That is kind of an oxymoron isn't it? Do they want me to lose more money? Are they really looking out for seniors or are they looking out for brokerage firms? Who spends the money on advertising that gives the financial press their job? Brokerage firms provide all the money. Open up any financial magazine if you do not believe me. By the way, how is your big brokerage firm doing for you these days?

Another thing that drives me crazy is this obsession over surrender charges. Annuities have payout options, one of which is called a period certain annuity payout. In our state Florida, you can annuitize a 12 year surrender charge annuity contract into a 5 year period certain annuity payout after just one year! In other words, you can get all your money back in 6 years. You can take a 10% free withdrawal out first, and then annuitize the other 90% over the next five years without penalty! This means take the balance in five annual installments. The surrender charge is irrelevant in this situation because it never comes into play with this type of planning.

Have you ever heard of Section 72(t) and 72(q) of the Internal Revenue Code? Come on tell the truth. Did you really know what 72(q) was? Most people have not heard about it. Section 72(q) is if you need to withdraw money from a Non-Qualified Annuity. Section 72(t) is if you need to withdraw money from an IRA or 403(b) annuity. If you have money in a Non-Qualified or Qualified Annuity and you are also under age 59 ½, then you can use these little known rules to get money out of your annuity(s) without the 10% early withdrawal penalty. You would still owe the taxes on the withdrawals, but you should not have to pay any surrender penalties or the 10% early withdrawal penalty in doing so. The major point here is no surrender penalties and no 10% early withdrawal penalties. You need a professional to help you decipher this area, however.

Well, I just told you how you could get out of most any annuity without surrender charges by utilizing the period certain feature of all annuity contracts. I also told you exactly what your risk on the downside would be if you had to cash in your annuity. This is certainly not true with regard to the stock market. You have no idea what the value of your stock market account will be in the future when you need the funds.

Some other ill-informed advisors say annuities are bad because they are subject to ordinary income taxes. Mutual funds largely are also subject to ordinary income taxes with some capital gains spun off each year, too. You have absolutely no control whatsoever over the tax implications of your mutual funds. There are not many investments out there that are not subject to ordinary income taxes, except stocks. Didn't I just explain the non-guaranteed nature of stocks?

If the regulators really wanted to, they could limit the commissions on the products that they approve. In addition, they could make sure all annuities have 5 year period certain clauses in their contracts that they approve. Further, they could limit surrender charges to reasonable terms. All of this is within their control on the front end during the approval process. If they established these guidelines in the beginning, it appears to me that they would save themselves a whole lot of regulatory headaches.

Uniformity is the answer folks. After all, mutual funds are regulated in this way. If a mutual fund company wants to sell its Class A share Equity Fund, then the commission charged is 5.75%. All fund companies can only do the same. They can charge less if they want to, but not more.

My suggestion is to make all annuities have a similar limit. Uniformity across the board is the solution. Is there anybody listening? Establish front load, back end load, level load and no load annuities. Make them uniform across the board on commissions and surrender charges. Then, all this abuse would significantly decrease. Until this happens, nothing is going to change. I say let us make it happen.

Imagine a world if you will where all annuities at most have six-year surrender charge. Then, it would be very clear to anyone offered an annuity that they would have at most a six-year surrender charge. In addition, there should be a maximum commission charge for annuities. The other thing uniformity would do is clear up all the major differences between annuities. This would make insurance companies who offer annuities compete on the annuity's performance. Now, that is a novel idea!

The way it stands now, you almost have to understand Egyptian hieroglyphics to interpret some of the annuities that are being sold today. It is really a simple solution that should clean up the bogus annuity peddlers out there while at the same time, make our friendly regulator's job easier.

My Idea for Mortgage Reform

I believe that I have a nice solution for the new Congress. They should pass legislation where everyone in America who has equity in their home can qualify for a home equity line worth the amount of their original down payment if they lose their job or become disabled. Boy that was a mouthful.

Homeowners should be allowed to access this home equity line of credit equal to their down payment, when they lose their a job, or become disabled. This would allow someone who lost their job, the time to find a new job and not lose their home in the process. If you became disabled, at least you would have some time to prepare your home for sale rather than go through the foreclosure process. It is kind of like a Home Equity Line of Credit using the down payment, but without having to qualify for it based on income.

The bankers of course will not like this idea, but I believe that they have proved beyond a shadow of a doubt here in 2008 that they do not know their $*#%@ from deep center field. Wouldn't you agree? Oh yes, they will tell you that they are good at managing money. They proved their incompetence to me. How about you?

My idea is that we all should have the ability to access our down payment in the case of job loss or disability. Granted, you would have to have equity in your house in the first place, but normal people put ten or twenty percent down, so this should not be a problem. By the way, maybe we need to go back to requiring twenty percent down. I have had to do that before on my home. If we reinstitute that requirement, wouldn't that automatically improve the quality of the loans on the books? It would get rid of the speculators too.

Without my idea, if you lose your job or get disabled, then you only have about 90 days before you lose your home. Although, some states like California and Florida have put moratoriums on foreclosures lately. All this will do is delay the inevitable. It is not a good idea in my book, literally. I think my approach is better.

Banks would totally be against this, of course. After all, assume that you paid extra on your house for years and you only owed about 30% of the value. If you lost your job and you did not already have a home equity line of credit outstanding, then the bank is going to get your house, with your entire pre-paid principal. Do you think that a bank is more likely to seize a house with a lot of equity in it or a little equity in it? Think about it. They have less of their money at risk in this situation. This is another reason not to plow extra money into your house. You are in a better negotiating position if you have very little equity in your house.

If you are disabled or lose your job, then you are screwed. Unless of course you bought disability insurance or find a job quickly. At a bare minimum, you ought to look at disability insurance to at least cover your mortgage, taxes and utilities on your house, if nothing else. If you have disability at work, get it.

As an investor, there are a lot of pitfalls and people out there who want to take your money away from you, including banks and mortgage lenders. It is very, very important that you are diligent in how you invest and how you pay the mortgage.

Here are the nuts and bolts of my ideas for the housing crisis:

The American Shared Appreciation Plan (ASAP)

Before ASAP – The Crisis Situation Today

Example Distressed Homeowner –

$400,000 - Original Home Value

$40,000 - Original Down Payment by Homeowner

$360,000 - Original Mortgage   *$250,000 – Current Appraised Home Value*

$2,158.38 - Monthly payment @ 6%   *$150,000 – Loss in Home Value*

There is a substantial risk of foreclosure with homeowners who are in similar predicaments. The mortgage lender is facing a minimum loss of $150,000. This risk could be higher due to the forced sales situation, continued property values declining, sales costs and other economic factors.

After Implementation of the American Shared Appreciation Plan (ASAP)

Refinance $400,000 property with $150,000 contribution from FNMA/FRE, $25,000 of original down payment from borrower and new mortgage from mortgage lender for $225,000.

Example:
1. $250,000 Currently Appraised Home Value
2. *$225,000 New Mortgage – Mortgage lender's new risk*
3. $25,000 Homeowner Equity
     a. Homeowner's equity is limited to 10% of the new appraised value or less depending on the original down payment by homeowner.
4. Homeowner gets a line of credit access to this equity *in case of job loss or total disability.*
     a. Homeowner can only access this line of credit with proof of job loss or disability. The disability to the homeowner must be certified by two doctors to last six months or longer.

      b.   Homeowner loses $15,000 in home equity in this example ($40,000 original down payment - $25,000 new homeowner equity) with the ASAP. Equity capped at 10%.

      c.   Homeowner can only use this line of credit to make house payments, pay homeowner's insurance and real estate taxes on the property. (Property related expenses.)

5. New loan - $1,348.99 Monthly payment @ 6% = $809.39 - Savings to Homeowner <u>per month</u>.

6. *$150,000 First Lien owed to FNMA/FRE - (ASAP) American Shared Appreciation Plan – Callable Discount Agency Notes (DAN's)*

      a. $150,000 is removed from Lender's Balance Sheet with the assumption by FNMA/FRE.

      b.   FNMA/FRE receives first lien, not the mortgage lender.

      c.   PMI is required on <u>all loans</u> in this plan to cover lenders risk on the new mortgage of $225,000. PMI costs are added to monthly payment.

      d.   If Homeowner pays off the mortgage, the first lien balance owed is still paid to FNMA/FRE when property is sold.

      e.   Potential debit to mortgage lender, but can be partially offset by purchase of DAN's that accrue interest payable to FNMA/FRE.

      f.   Homeowner still stands to benefit because they will receive exactly what they would have received if they bought a $250,000 home. The fact that FNMA/FRE has a first lien is irrelevant to homeowner. It only affects the mortgage lender.

      g.   Callable Discount Notes are sold in the bond marketplace to help offset initial costs of $150,000 assumption by FNMA/FRE. For example, 5.49% DAN's, sold to an investor at present value of the loan term. $30,182.31 is the cost to investor for the DAN that matures at $150,000 in 30 years. Accrued interest for DAN's accrues to investor.

      h.   Lender is required to purchase DAN's. Interest accrues to FNMA/FRE *and not to lender.* Theoretically, if DAN is held to maturity, then $150,000 is paid back to FNMA/FRE.

      i.   DAN's can be traded on the secondary market like regular FNMA/FRE agencies.

j.   Only FHA approved mortgage lenders are allowed to participate.

*Interest assumptions are based on an annual crediting method for illustration purposes.

Benefits of ASAP – Win for Homeowners – Win for Lender – Win for Taxpayers

1. This takes the risk of the $150,000 loss off the Mortgage lender's balance sheet. Cost to Lender is the initial cost of the DAN's (In this example, it is $30,182.31.) and the loss of accrued interest.
2. Homeowner saves $809.39 per month in mortgage payment. (must add PMI costs)
3. Homeowner retains a portion ($25,000) of their home equity (10% limit) with the right to access upon job loss or disability. These features should keep homeowners from walking away.
    a.   New mortgage loans should have these features to spur housing demand.
4. Homeowner can stay in home, and build home equity as if they bought a $250,000 home.
5. PMI covers Lender's risk for the newly restructured loan.
6. If house is paid off after 30-year loan period or earlier then mortgage lender pays FNMA/FRE the balance of the $150,000 minus the cost of the DAN and accrued interest. Lender is required to fund this liability with a Callable Discount Agency Note at closing.
7. ASAP covers the taxpayer's/FNMA/FRE with a first lien upon the sale of the property.
8. Homeowner is third in line, but is in the same position as if they bought a $250,000 home.
    a.   Let's assume the property is sold for $400,000 ten years later. After paying FNMA/FRE back the balance of the $150,000, the homeowner would still net $250,000 plus the difference in accrued interest paid back to FNMA/FRE by the lender.
9. Property Values should stabilize thus turning around our economy.
10. $150,000 Callable Discount Agency Notes could be sold by FNMA/FRE. Suggestion would be to structure like a callable zero coupon note based on the term of the loan. Use current market rates.

a. For example, 5.49% rate of interest, sold at present value of $30,182.31, matures in 30 years at $150,000.00. (Annual rate.)

    i. Mortgage lenders should be required buyers of this to pre-fund their liabilities.

    ii. Bond investors would buy these DAN's and a secondary market would exist.

    iii. Extra funds received by bond investors should help FNMA/FRE with cash flow.

b. FNMA/FRE receives $30,182.31 upon sale of Discount Agency Note. If house is sold before 30 years, then FNMA/FRE receives balance of $150,000 and the Discount Agency Note is called. FNMA/FRE is in effect is receiving the present value of $150,000 which should mean <u>minimal cost to taxpayers.</u>

    i. Example of house sold at a loss:

        1. House sold 3 years later for $200,000 ($50,000 loss from ASAP loan of $250,000.)

        2. FNMA/FRE received $30,182.31 initially at loan closing from lender.

        3. FNMA/FRE receives $97,417.99, which is $150,000 - $30,182.31 minus 3 years of accrued interest on the DAN at closing. ($22,399.70)

        4. Mortgage lender receives $102,582.01 after paying balance of $150,000 to FNMA/FRE.

            a. Net cost to Mortgage lender is $47,417.99 three years from now.

            b. Mortgage lenders would want to go after homeowner for the $47,417.99 loss in home value, but I say the lenders need to be penalized for causing the housing crisis. Lesson learned, hopefully.

            c. Leave homeowners alone who worked within the confines of the ASAP and do not allow Mortgage lenders to sue them if the house loses value after the ASAP loan. *This will keep homeowners from walking away if they do not have this worry.*

    d. This is significantly better for the Mortgage lenders than $150,000 or more loss today.

  5. Homeowner receives $0.00 since their house was sold at a loss. This is the same situation that they would have been in, if they bought a $250,000 home and later sold it for $200,000.

  c. Investor who buys Callable Discount Agency Note would have received 5.49% (currently declared rate) in interest for as long as they held the Callable Discount Agency Note.

    i. FNMA/FRE calls the Discount Agency Note for investors when the corresponding mortgage transaction is closed out.

Other Details of the ASAP

1. No interest earnings on the $150,000 for FNMA/FRE, but Callable Discount Agency Notes could be sold to raise funds from the bond marketplace. $150,000 paid to the mortgage lender to remove from their balance sheet, but actual net assumption by FNMA/FRE in the above example is $119,817.69 assuming they receive the lender proceeds from sale of the DAN's.

  a. In addition, sales of DAN's to bond marketplace would reduce FNMA/FRE's initial outlay. There would be an interest cost for the DAN's to FNMA/FRE, but this is better than just printing money.

2. Lender owes FNMA/FRE $150,000 via the first lien. Cost of DAN's to mortgage lender is to pre-fund liability to FNMA/FRE. The $30,182.31 that accrues interest to pay back FNMA/FRE for the lender is a whole lot better than $150,000 or more cost to lender today.

3. Lender has a second lien on the property. – This is their penalty for causing the crisis. Lender only receives interest from borrower on the new ASAP loan. Lender can spread their risk over life of the loan by purchasing DAN's. Also, covered by PMI.

4. In the case of foreclosure with the newly restructured loan, the lender is no worse off than before the crisis. However,

the foreclosure rate should return to normal levels after the implementation of the ASAP, the lender's purchase of DAN's and the sales in the bond marketplace of the DAN's to investors. The ASAP benefits homeowners and provides much needed solution.

I trust you will agree that these ideas make sense. There is good and bad in there, I know, but instead of the government shouldering the whole burden, I have it where everyone involved shoulders some of the burden. You have to make it appeal to all parties in my opinion. Otherwise, it will not work.

New Paradigm

During the Great Depression, banks and stock brokerages were all tied together. Back then, a bank could call your loan due at any time. There was no protection for the borrower. Hence, this is the reason we were all taught to find a good job and pay off our home as fast as you can. Your home was not safely yours unless you paid it off. After the Great Depression, Congress changed the laws and separated the banks and stock brokerage firms, so the next time there was a run on the banks it would not affect people who had money in the stock market, or at insurance companies. At least that was the thought process.

Do you watch PBS? If so, you may want to watch their documentary on the Great Depression. It is fascinating to watch. I bet you can call your local PBS station and order a copy of it on DVD. It would be worth it if you did. Give them an extra donation while you are at it, too.

Fast forward, if you will to the year 1999. The Glass-Steagall Act was repealed by the Gramm, Leach, and Bliley Act. The Glass Steagall Act was the act that Congress passed to keep banks separate from investment firms and insurance companies. The banks lobbied hard because people were taking money out of banks in droves and putting it in mutual funds and insurance products. Ever since the repeal of the Glass-Steagall Act, you can walk into any bank and buy CD's, stocks, bonds or insurance. Further, you can walk into any investment firm and buy a CD, stocks, bonds or insurance. In addition, you can walk into any insurance office and buy CD's, stocks, bonds or insurance. Funny how they are all selling the same thing, isn't it?

Today, they all want to be bank holding companies so they can get some of the free billions that the government is passing out. My opinion is the government needs to stay out of the free markets. Do not get me started on that. My book might be 900 pages long if I went down that path.

Bailouts and Slush Funds

Citi Group recently was fined along with UBS for hawking those Auction Rate Preferred's that I mentioned early in the book. Morgan Stanley had to buy back from investors several billion dollars worth of these securities.

Well, guess what? The taxpayers are paying the fine for Citi now, because they requested $45 billion of TARP money from the government to bailout them out. Now let me get this straight. Citi had to buy back billions of dollars of these ARS's, then we as the taxpayers have to pay their fine? Something does not seem right about that to me. How about you?

All options are on the table in this crazy year of government bailouts, bank slush funds and my personal favorite, bridge loans. I am sure that Congress will give the auto industry a bridge loan to nowhere. Do not get me wrong. I want GM, Ford and Chrysler all to make it. They just need to make it as every other company in America has done in hard times. No freebies for bad union contracts and bad management decisions. It is sad but true that Chapter 11 needs to happen. Perhaps, they need to break up GM and let Cadillac and Chevrolet stand on their own.

I want to see the new Chevy Camaro myself, so I hope everything works out. I cannot wait to see the new Ford Mustang either. I rented a Chrysler Sebring the other day and I was impressed. It was a very nice vehicle. Surely, these people can solve these problems for themselves. Americans still love their cars. There is always a plan and a process for success. Let us hope they roll up their sleeves, knuckle down, and get it done.

You must understand that there is a lot of posturing going on in the Auto industry mêlée. After all, the UAW leaders are probably the best negotiators in the country. They are telling these Congressmen and Congresswomen that had better do X Y and Z or there will be hell to pay. In reality, it is just a massive sales job on America that is going on. Like I said earlier, just go to Chapter 11 and get on with it.

Celebrate!

Life is short. Celebrate. September 11, 2001 changed our lives forever. It should also have changed how you look at being *aggressive*. The year 2008 confirmed to us that we cannot wholly rely on the stock market for our futures. Can you really assume that holding 80 to 100% stocks will be a smart thing to do going forward? I could be wrong, but I do not think so.

We all cannot be rich. There is something inherently noble by just being a firefighter or a police officer as the events of September 11 have shown us. Look at how the first responders reacted to the US Air plane landing in the Hudson River. The crew on that airplane performed in a courageous manner as did the first responders on the scene. These people are real heroes.

I have a friend who is a firefighter and in the Army National Guard. He just went to Iraq for you and me. His name is Eric Lamm and he is top notch. This person is good as gold and has a great family. Eric calls to tell me that he is looking for clients for me and wants more of my business cards. What a guy! He humbles me into believing that I must be doing something right.

A young woman that I go to church with, Suzanne Openshaw is in the military and just went to Iraq, again for you and me. She did this with four young children at home! Do you really understand the sacrifices that these great Americans are making on our behalf? I had to tell her when she made it back, "Thank you for your service to our country". You need to do that when you talk to our military heroes. They need to hear it. It means a lot to them.

Look at our young men and women in the military in Iraq, Afghanistan and around the world. They are risking their lives so you and I can live in freedom. I do not know about you, but I will never forget the sacrifice that they made for my family. I know the awful pain of losing a son and my heart goes out to the families of our military men and women killed in action.

Thank God that you are an American. Do the best that you can with whatever talents that God has blessed upon you. Try to improve yourself along the way. You will be much happier, believe me.

I believe it is a safe assumption that we have even less visibility into the future today than we had before September 11, 2001. Look at the recent event in Mumbai India where many innocents were killed. The terrorists have not gone away. They still want to kill us and wreck our economy and other economies in the world.

Our military has done an exceptional job in Afghanistan and Iraq. We have made great strides with heroic sacrifices to make the world a safer place. We have attacked terrorism head on, but perhaps we could all agree that some measure of uncertainty lies ahead. I am not advocating that you freeze up and not invest at all. My position is to move away from that *aggressive* stance. Join the AIA (Aggressive Investor's Anonymous.) I do not know if we have an organization like this, but I certainly know many people who need to attend it.

If you stay out there on that jagged edge, then you are going to step on something sharp and it is going to be painful. Do not get caught up in the rat race of chasing performance. It is a loser's game. You need to focus on your family and friends and you do that by not being *aggressive*.

Do a little Financial planning. Break your goals and objectives down to reasonable ones that are truly attainable. Work on one goal or objective at a time. Invest the money for each to accomplish that goal or objective. Then, repeat the process for each goal or objective. Keep in mind the 20%/65% rule.

Imagine how you will feel every time that you attain one of your goals. Your three year goal to set aside "x" number of dollars….*achieved*. Your six-year goal….*achieved*. Your ten-year goal….*achieved*. Wouldn't it be nice to have had a portfolio of investments during your lifetime that has been filled with successes?

Here are my wishes for you: I wish that you have the freedom to live, as you desire. I wish that you have comfort in knowing that your financial strategy will give you the financial security that you are seeking. I wish that you obtain balance in your life. I wish that you have more time for your friends and family. I hope that you help other people through charitable endeavors. Perhaps, the most important thing is that you become closer to Jesus Christ.

Above all, be happy with who you are and let other people do the envying. Make a commitment to yourself and your family to never be *aggressive* again. Be vigilant, dedicated and disciplined, and then you will be successful. In addition, do not forget your spiritual relationship.

THE STREAK - CAN YOUR FINANCIAL ADVISOR DO THIS?

For the last twenty-one years, I have played in the Men's Senior Baseball League World Series in Phoenix, Arizona each fall. I love the Phoenix area and look forward to my annual baseball pilgrimage. Yes, that is right. I am 52 years old and still play baseball. I was the leadoff man for our team this past October.

Each year, I meet up with my Arkansas friends to play baseball at this national tournament. We have had tremendous success out there. I cannot even remember all the times we have made it to the Final 4. In addition, we have had several opportunities to win it all, but have always managed to end up in second place. Nevertheless, we have a blast and keep trying each year.

About five years ago, I had a streak at the plate that was truly special. We play six games guaranteed and then advance to the playoffs depending on our Division record. The six games are played within four days. During this week of baseball, I began a hitting streak where I reached base safely nineteen (19) times in a row! Not games in a row, but at bats in a row! During this streak, I hit one inside the park home run, had two triples, two doubles, and ten singles, was hit by the pitcher twice and walked twice. I faced fifteen different pitchers from the teams that I faced that week. It did not matter who they threw at me. I got on base anyway. How did I do it? I listened to disco all week on XM Satellite Radio. The channel of my motivation was the Chrome station. It puts out Disco 24/7. It fired me up. My roommate, Jimmy "Bum" Scott kept me in the zone.

By the way, there is no personality on the planet like Jimmy Scott. He is a great person and a ton of fun to be around. Right before I left for this last Phoenix trip, he called and asked, "How fat are you?" I cracked up laughing. He is hilarious to be around, believe me.

After the tournament ended, I was written up in Hardball Magazine for my efforts. As I said, can your financial advisor do that? That is what I thought!

Conclusion

We covered many different topics in this book. Some of the ideas were simple and some were complex. I would like for you to consider this book as a reference source. When you need help with regard to Liabilities, then open the book and re-read the Liability Planning section. This way, you will be sure and get the major points related to Liability Planning or whichever section of the book that you re-read.

There are some major points that I want you to walk away with in taking the time to read this book. I have summarized them here for you.

1. Understand what type of financial advisor you are doing business with or that you are contemplating doing business with.
2. Do a background check on your financial advisor, even if you do not think it is necessary. This includes me.
3. Know all the compensation methods that you will be exposed to with your financial advisor.
4. Be vigilant against situations that may seem outside the norm with regard to where your assets are held, or managed. No secrets allowed!
5. Use a financial advisor who uses a reputable custodian for your accounts like Charles Schwab & Co. Inc.
6. Understand the process that your financial advisor uses to make investment decisions.
7. Use the 20%/65% Rule <u>at all times</u>.
8. Do not be afraid to go to cash.
9. Know when to hire a professional financial advisor.
10. Work in conjunction with your financial advisor in developing a Comprehensive Financial Plan.
11. Make smart decisions with regard to your liabilities.

12. Use the 20%/65% Rule for your retirement plans.
13. Consider the tax implications of everything that you own when you are in retirement. Look for ways to reduce taxes and increase your income.
14. Do not pay tax on income that you do not need.
15. Know that there is a 0% capital gains tax if your AGI is under $65,100 in 2009.
16. Consider LTC alternatives like Hybrid Life or Hybrid Annuities with LTC riders.
17. If you are a business owner, obtain Business Overhead Expense insurance and Disability Buy Out insurance if you have a partner.
18. Put all Life Insurance policies in Irrevocable Life Insurance Trusts.
19. If you are married, split your assets in order to take advantage of the Estate Tax Exemption.
20. Give more to your favorite charity. The money you have is a gift from God.
21. For larger estates, consider the Zeroed Out 2 Year Rolling GRAT.
22. Consider the Installment Sales Trust to defer capital gains taxes on real property.
23. Use a short-term loan from a Home Equity Line of Credit, a Reverse Mortgage, or the EquityKey Real Estate Option to pay the taxes on your IRA conversion.
24. Know how to buy a house, if you are age 62 or older with the Reverse Mortgage (HECM) Purchase program.
25. Use ETF's or Exchange Traded Funds to diversify your portfolio instead of high expense Mutual Funds and Variable Annuities.
26. Consider the use of Single Premium Immediate Annuities for income and Fixed Annuities for Growth. Both of which are guaranteed by the insurance companies who offer them.
27. Finally, live to please God, not yourself.

About the Author's Business

A Plug for Me is a Plug for You

Comprehensive Financial Planning is what your expectation should be for a relationship with a financial advisor or financial planner. I am able to offer you those services. I am not looking to build the biggest firm in the country, but I like working with a select group of people who like advanced financial planning that looks at all aspects of your financial life. That is assets *and* liabilities for you folks in Rio Linda.

I am a real financial planner with the designations, and the experience to go with. If you can come see me, (or one of the advisors who I teach) for the value that we bring to the table, then why would you go anywhere else? Investment counseling should come with no hidden agendas and transparency when it comes to conflicts of interest.

Is this financial planning thing sinking in yet? I hope so. This is the future my friends. Come see me, or one of the professionals like me who are smart enough to build their business around a similar model. No *undisclosed* conflicts of interest and no hidden agendas are what we offer. Transparency is the name of the game today.

My personal company slogan is *Keep Your Assets. Take My Advice,* which is the same title as my book. I hope you like it. Please feel free to visit my Web site at http://www.firstcoastplanning.com. You can also e-mail me from that Web site and give me your thoughts on my book. Thank you very much. God Bless you and yours. Read your Bible and say your prayers and I will do the same.

Glossary

Business Overhead Expense Insurance - This is a type of disability policy that pays benefits for a business owner's expenses in the case of their disability.

CCRC - Continuing Care Retirement Community. A place where seniors can buy into to live out their lives that provides lifestyle activities while they are healthy and medical care, as they get older.

Charitable Lead Trust - Where a gift of an income stream is given to a charitable and is deductible as a charitable contribution for as long as the donor lives. At death, the principal is passed to family members and the income stream to the charity ceases.

Charitable Remainder Trust - Where a gift of assets (the principal) is given to a trust for an immediate tax deduction against adjusted gross income. The income from the gift is paid to the donor for the period chosen and is taxable to the donor.

Core & Satellite - A form of diversification that says to put the majority of your assets in a broadly diversified index fund (core), and then builds other alternative investments (satellite) around the core.

Custodians - Firms like Charles Schwab & Co. Inc., Fidelity (National Financial Services), TD Ameritrade, Scottrade, and others who hold the assets of clients of registered investment advisers.

Disability Buy Out Insurance - This disability policy provides the funds in case a business partner becomes disabled. It acts as a buy sell agreement for disability.

EquityKey Real Estate Option - A real estate option that is taxed when the option is sold, exercised or lapses. The EquityKey Real Estate Option provides a debt free payment to the homeowner in exchange for a share of the future appreciation of the property.

Estate Splitting - This is the strategy to have individually owned assets for husbands and wives who are over the estate tax threshold. The advantage is that if one spouse were to die, then their individually owned assets placed in a Bypass Trust would not be subject to the estate tax.

ETF's - Exchange Traded Funds. Investments by firms such as iShares, Vanguard, State Street Global Research, Powershares, ProShares, Rydex, Wisdom Tree, Claymore and others that trade on an exchange and are generally based on an underlying index, either long or short. Typically, ETF's have lower operating expenses than mutual funds in the same asset class.

FINRA - The Financial Industry Regulatory Association. The regulator for registered representatives who work on behalf of their broker/ dealer.

HECM - A reverse mortgage. A reverse mortgage allows for either an income stream or a line of credit to homeowners age 62 or older that is paid back normally at the death of the homeowner. Reverse mortgages are typically used to help supplement a senior's income in retirement and are considered a last resort option.

HECM Purchase Program - A new program effective January 1, 2009 that allows homeowners age 62 or older to purchase a new home and immediately take out a reverse mortgage on it, in order to avoid mortgage payments.

Hybrid Life with LTC Rider - This is a single premium life insurance contract with a long-term care insurance rider. This product functions as a single premium life insurance contract with a death benefit if the insured lives and never needs long term care. It functions as a long-term care policy that pays tax-free benefits if the insured were to need long-term care.

Hybrid Annuity with LTC Rider - This is a fixed annuity with a long-term care rider. This product functions as a fixed annuity with guaranteed rate of interest if the annuitant lives and never needs long term care. It functions as a long-term care policy that pays tax-free benefits if the insured were to need long-term care.

ILIT - An irrevocable life insurance trust that has a purpose of removing the ownership of a life insurance on the insured from the estate of the insured for estate tax purposes.

Installment Sales Trust - This strategy is based on Section 453 of the Internal Revenue Code. It allows for the deferral of capital gains taxes for the sale of property.

IPS - Investment Policy Statement. A process form that establishes the groundwork for an investment plan. It includes time horizon, risk tolerances, return expectations, investment exclusions, and rebalancing requirements.

Living Trust - A revocable trust designed to spell out the grantor's intentions for the disposition of assets owned by the grantor, at the grantor's death. Assets in a Living Trust bypass the probate process.

Margin - This is a loan on brokerage account assets. Typically, you can borrow up to 50% of the value of your stocks (immediately) and mutual funds (after 30 days) in order to solve short-term cash flow needs. Sometimes used as leverage to buy more stocks, but this is a risky strategy.

Model Portfolios - Industry jargon for sample investment portfolios showing how a financial advisor or financial services firm might invest your assets. Typical Model Portfolios range from Conservative, Moderate, and Aggressive.

Monte Carlo Simulation - A software program that runs numerous iterations in order to determine what the potential for success is of a given mix of assets.

Period Certain Payout - A feature of an annuity that guarantees a payment for the period chosen. A 5-year period certain would return your principal in five years with interest declared by the insurance company.

RMD's - Required Minimum Distributions. Beginning by April 1 of the year following you turning 70 1/2, you are required to begin taking distributions from your IRA or other retirement plan.

Roth IRA Conversion - The process of taking a Traditional IRA and converting it to a Roth IRA in order to take advantage of the tax free nature of Roth IRA's.

SEC - The United States Securities and Exchange Commission. The federal regulator for registered investment adviser firms. They also regulate mutual funds and publicly traded companies.

Single Premium Immediate Annuities - Instruments guaranteed by the full faith and credit of the insurance company issuing it. They provide various payout options from period certain time periods like 5 or 10 year, up to lifetime payout periods.

Stretch IRA - The terminology used to stretch your IRA to your spouse and children over their lifetimes. Each beneficiary takes a required minimum distribution based on his or her personal life expectancy.

The 20/65% Rule - The strategy presented by the author of this book that recommends that an investor puts no more than 20% into any one asset class and no more than 65% in stocks or stock investments such as mutual funds, variable annuity sub-accounts or Exchange Traded Funds.

Zeroed Out 2 Year Rolling GRAT - A Grantor Retained Annuity Trust that is paid to the grantor in two annual payments with the Section 7520 declared interest rate. Any earnings over and above the Section 7520 interest rate, remains in the trust for the benefit of the beneficiary and is gift tax-free.

www.ingramcontent.com/pod-product-compliance
Lightning Source LLC
Chambersburg PA
CBHW032008170526
45157CB00002B/593